COOKING WITH
GRAINS

BY
SUSAN SLACK

ILLUSTRATIONS BY
MICHELLE BURCHARD

HPBooks
a division of
PRICE STERN SLOAN
Los Angeles

Cover photo by Glenn Cormier Photography
Published by HPBooks
a division of Price Stern Sloan, Inc.
11150 Olympic Boulevard
Los Angeles, California 90064
© 1993 Susan Slack
Illustrations and cover photo © 1993 Price Stern Sloan, Inc.

Library of Congress Cataloging-in-Publication Data
Slack, Susan Fuller.
   Cooking with grains / by Susan Slack ; illustrations by Michelle Burchard.
    p.   cm.
   Includes index
   ISBN 1-55788-079-4 (acid-free paper) : $8.95
   1. Cookery (Cereals) I. Title.
 TX808.S63 1993
 641.6'31—dc20   93-25574
                                                                 CIP

Printed in the U.S.A.

10 9 8 7 6 5 4 3 2 1

NOTICE: The information in this book is true and complete to the best of our knowledge. All recommendations are made without any guarantees on the part of the author or Price Stern Sloan. The author and publisher disclaim all liability in connection with the use of this information.

This book is printed on acid-free paper.

Acknowledgments

I would like to say thank you to several companies for providing research materials and grains to help me with the development of many recipes in this book; Deborah Locke, Texmati® Brand Rice Products, Alvin, Texas; Mike Davis, Conrad Rice Mill Inc., New Iberia, Louisiana; Arrowhead Mills, Hereford, Texas; Martha Johnson, Eden Foods, Clinton, Michigan; Lundberg Family Farms, Richvale, California; and Jack Kenward of the Rice Growers Association of California in Sacramento.

A special thank you to Editorial Director Jeanette Egan for her support, enthusiasm and superb organizational sense. I would also like to say thank you to Ara Burklund for her invaluable assistance on this book and for her cheerful and gracious disposition which is a constant joy.

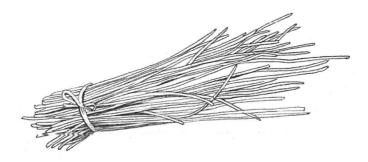

Contents

Introduction

A Brief History of Grains

The cereal grasses include wheat, corn, rice, oats, barley, millet, rye and grain sorghum. Other grain sources come from plants which are not grasses, such as buckwheat, amaranth and quinoa. They are harvested, prepared and eaten like grains from grass.

The birth of civilization was sparked around 9000 B.C. with the cultivation of a tall, wild wheat which still grows in the Far East along the fertile river deltas. Wild wheat had always been a source of sustenance for nomadic early man. As he roamed from place to place in search of food, chance encounters allowed him many opportunities to gather the nutritious wild seed. Eventually, man made a serendipitous discovery. He became aware that uneaten seed, discarded or spilled, would sprout from the earth the following year. Through much experimentation, he learned how to plant and cultivate the seeds. This enabled him to abandon the hunter-gatherer lifestyle and settle down close to his crops to await the harvest. Meat and fish were eaten whenever available, but grain became the basis of man's diet.

By 7000 B.C., domesticated wheat is believed to have been growing abundantly in the Tigris-Euphrates Valley. Barley was domesticated for human consumption around 6000 B.C. The foundation of most ancient cooking was based on grains. At first, the grains were simply roasted and eaten. Later their flavor and digestibility were improved, when man began cooking them in water to produce a type of gruel. Early loaves of flat bread probably evolved from portions of the thick gruel dried on hot stones. Around 3000 B.C. bakers stumbled upon the process of fermentation, and breads eventually became lighter and softer. In addition to fermentation and leavening, the Egyptians invented clay ovens.

Many thriving cultures base their entire existence upon grain production. Wheat has been grown in the Middle East for thousands of years. Whole-wheat berries are cooked and eaten, or parched and processed into a type of cracked wheat called bulgur. An important part of the daily Middle Eastern diet, bulgur is soaked for salads, cooked like pilaf or added to soups. In Italy, the endosperm of hard durum wheat is ground into golden semolina, the basic ingredient for dried Italian pasta. Couscous, also made from semolina, is a grainlike starch central to the diet of North Africa. The word couscous encompasses an entire category of dishes which includes the steamed grain as well as cooked meats and vegetables.

Since China's early history, the centerpiece of each meal has been a bowl of rice. Diners add flavor to the plain rice with a diverse assortment of well-seasoned vegetables and a small amount of meat. For centuries, the rhythms of daily life in Japan have revolved around the planting and harvesting of rice. There is even an official table etiquette which prescribes the proper method for eating the grain. Rice is also a staple food in Korea, but barley and millet are often added to the rice pot. Far Eastern diners know that grains served in a rice bowl can be conveniently scooped directly into the mouth with the use of chopsticks. The sticky texture of Asian rice is also a boon when using chopsticks.

In North America, the favorite rice has long been the fluffy, long-grain Indica-type rice. Rice farming began in South Carolina around the 1680s with seed brought by ship from Madagascar. We are discovering American adaptations of Asian rice such as Louisiana Wild Pecan Rice and Wehani® rice, Texmati® rice and sushi rice from California. They are a blend of the best qualities of our domestic varieties with some of the flavors and textures of the more exotic imported types. Wild rice, an indigenous American grass, grows abundantly in lakes and lowlands. Wild rice requires longer cooking than brown rice, and triples in bulk when cooked.

In India, few meals are complete without a serving of grains in one form or another. They provide the vast vegetarian population with an affordable source of protein and calories. Barley, rice, buckwheat, grain sorghum, wheat and corn are an integral part of the Indian diet. In the northern regions of India and China, millet and wheat are widely grown and eaten. Breads are an important food in these northern diets, much like rice is in other regions.

Corn, or maize, another native American grain, has been a very significant plant. Archeological findings in Central America show corn was a hybrid devised through centuries of cross-breeding of native grasses. It is probably the most versatile of all the grains in the world today.

In Mexico, corn is processed and ground into masa, a corn dough used for making many dishes, including the tortilla, the mainstay of the Mexican diet. North American Indians use a similar process to produce hominy and grits which involves soaking dried corn in water and wood ash. Dried corn is also ground into coarse meal for making breads and puddings. These native foods are important components of the American diet today. In mountainous Northern Italy, cornmeal is also a staple, cooked into a thick, delicious porridge called polenta. Corn, cooked into a thin porridge, is the basis of many peasant diets and is often substituted for bread.

The "new grains," amaranth, quinoa, millet, spelt and kamut, have actually been around for centuries. Native to Mexico and the Andes Mountains of South America, amaranth and quinoa are regarded as nutritional "supergrains." They contain high amounts of the eight essential amino acids which form a complete protein, including lysine, which is usually deficient in grains.

Grains are often ground into flour for making bread. Flour and water are the two basic bread ingredients; other ingredients such as leavening, eggs, salt and sugar improve the bread's texture, flavor and appearance. A portion of flour from other grains such as rye, buckwheat, triticale, oats, rice or cornmeal can be blended with wheat flour to create breads with interesting flavors and textures. Cooked whole grains such as rice, millet or quinoa add rustic texture and earthy flavor to breads.

As you can see, for many countries throughout the world, grains are the heart of most meals. In fact, a large number of the religions of these countries honor a goddess of the grain.

Today, when we walk into supermarkets and health food stores, we can find many of the less familiar grains and flours which our international friends have been eating for centuries. In the interest of good health, it is time to include them on our pantry shelf beside our old favorites.

A Guide to Good Health

We all consume the seeds of various cereal grasses in our daily diets without giving it much thought. We might begin the day with hot oatmeal or corn flakes, then grab a sandwich made with hearty rye or whole-wheat bread for lunch. In the evening, a side dish of rice or hominy grits might be found on the dinner plate, often overshadowed by a generous portion of meat. In the past, grains have played a secondary role in our Western society of meat-and-potatoes lovers, but the role of grains is changing fast. Recommendations from nutritional researchers encouraging us to increase the amount of grains and vegetables in our diets are well-founded; we are discovering that people who consume a plant-rich diet suffer from fewer chronic diseases. Nutritionists tell us these high-fiber foods provide significant amounts of protein, complex carbohydrates, vitamins, minerals and fiber—just what we need in our diets to help our bodies stave off digestive tract disorders, heart disease and cancer.

The foundation of the USDA's new Food Guide Pyramid is the Bread, Cereal, Rice and Pasta Group, clearly the largest of the four food groups from which we are encouraged to select our daily food servings. The concept is that we should choose more foods from the bottom of the pyramid than from those near the top. From the grain group, six to eleven servings are recommended each day. Typical serving sizes are one slice of bread or one muffin, one-half cup of cooked rice, barley or grits or one cup dry cereal. When planning your daily menus, begin with the grain group at the base of the pyramid and work your way up. Grains and grain-based foods should comprise the largest part of your diet, followed by fruits and vegetables.

Basic Recipes

This chapter is a collection of basic, easy recipes for cooking grains, including types of rice, wheat, barley and quinoa. Enjoy the simple, natural taste of these grains, perhaps seasoned with a little salt or butter. Their mild background flavors will compliment any ingredient or seasoning you might care to add. A brief perusal of the recipes in this book will illustrate the fact that grains are remarkably adaptable and can be used in a number of creative, delicious ways. Turn them into main dishes, side dishes, soups, salads, breads and desserts.

When cooking grains, it is important to select the correct pan. Choose a flat-bottomed pot made from a solid material such as anodized aluminum, heavy-gauge stainless steel or porcelain-clad metal. The pot must have a tight-fitting lid to retain moisture and heat. Use an appropriate size pot for the amount of grain you are cooking to prevent under-cooking or burning. A two-quart saucepan is ideal for cooking two cups of a raw grain. Delicate grain recipes such as polenta and rice pudding can be cooked in a double boiler to prevent burning. The Japanese rice cooker has a thermostatic control which turns off the heat when the rice is done. This has greatly simplified the chore of rice preparation, producing perfectly cooked rice every time.

If the grain is not tender and dry after the initial cooking time, re-cover the pot and cook five minutes longer. For more moist rice, add a little extra hot liquid while cooking; cold liquid will make the rice mushy. To prevent gumminess, never stir rice while it is cooking.

The moisture content of different types of rice varies, depending on the time of the harvest, the humidity, the age of the rice and even the method of cooking. New crop rice, called *shimnai* in Japan, requires less water than aged rice. Water amounts can be slightly adjusted as necessary.

Grain Storage

Grains, seeds and flours should always be stored in a cool dry place, out of direct sunlight, preferably at a temperature around 65°F (20°C). Properly stored, grains will stay in prime condition for six to nine months. To prevent bug infestation, store grains, seeds and flours in airtight containers in the refrigerator or in the freezer for longer-term storage. Quinoa, an oil-rich seed, is prone to spoilage. Buy it in small amounts; store in a clean glass jar in a cool, dry place or in the refrigerator. Oil-rich wheat germ, cornmeal and grits also spoil easily; store in a similar manner. When grains and seeds are past their prime, they will have a strong, rancid smell. Spoiled amaranth has a smell which resembles linseed oil. Whole-wheat flour is also highly susceptible to rancidity; refrigerate it in an airtight container.

Rice: To Rinse or Not to Rinse

Asian cooks perform the daily ritual of rinsing rice as a prelude to meal preparation. Rinsing removes milling impurities, bran residue, stones and insects. According to the American rice industry, it is not necessary to prerinse domestic rice. Thanks to advanced agricultural technology, rice is cleaner and more uniform than ever. In addition, nutrients included in the cornstarch-corn syrup topical coating on medi-um-grain California Calrose rice would be lost during rinsing.

Although technically unnecessary, custom often prevails and Asian cooks continue to rinse, whatever the type of rice. Having lived in Japan several years, I also rinse rice destined for Asian dishes. The fresh, clean taste of rinsed rice is perceptible, and this is especially important in Japanese cuisine, where the singular flavor of each food is appreciated on its own merits. If washing nutrients down the drain concerns you, follow the example of many Asian cooks and use the initial rinse water for making breads, soups, vegetables and other dishes.

To rinse rice for Asian or Indian dishes, cover the measured amount of rice with cool tap water in a large bowl. Gently swish the rice, rubbing it gently between your hands to remove powdery coatings. Pour off the milky water; add fresh water. Continue rinsing in this manner for three minutes or until the water runs almost clear. Drain rice in a fine strainer; tap off excess water. Follow each recipe's directions for soaking and cooking, as soaking produces a more tender grain. Rice is never rinsed after cooking.

BASIC BROWN RICE

Brown rice requires longer cooking than white rice because the bran layer is left intact. Lightly milled or light-bran rice is fluffier than regular brown rice and cooks in half the time.

1 cup long- or medium-grain brown rice
About 2-1/2 cups homemade stock (page 24), canned chicken broth or water

In a medium-size saucepan, combine rice and 2-1/4 cups stock. Bring to a boil. Cover pan with a tight-fitting lid. Reduce heat to low; simmer 45 to 50 minutes. Add additional stock, if needed. When rice is tender and liquid has been absorbed, remove from heat; let stand, undisturbed, 10 minutes. Makes 3 to 4 cups.

Variation

For 1 cup short-grain brown rice, reduce the amount of liquid to 2 cups.

SWEET GLUTINOUS RICE

These fat, chalky, grains of rice are so starchy that they lose their shape when cooked, becoming sticky and cohesive. Use sweet rice for Asian puddings, stuffings, dumplings, rice soup or sweet snacks.

1-1/2 cups sweet glutinous rice, rinsed as directed on page 12
Water

Soak rice in 3 cups water 2 hours or overnight. Drain rice; spread over a 9- or 10-inch shallow, heatproof pan. Sprinkle in 3 tablespoons water. In a wok or deep pot, bring 2 inches of water to a boil. Place pan of rice on a steamer tray; cover and place over boiling water. Steam 5 minutes. If rice is not tender, sprinkle with additional water and steam 5 minutes longer. Remove pan from steamer. Use rice as desired. Makes about 4-1/2 cups.

COOKED LONG-GRAIN RICE

*Long-grain rice, which cooks up dry and fluffy, is the rice preferred
by most Americans and Europeans.*

2 cups homemade stock (page 24), canned chicken broth or water
1 cup long-grain rice
1 tablespoon butter or margarine
1/4 to 1/2 teaspoon salt

In a medium-size saucepan over high heat, combine all ingredients. Bring to a boil. Reduce heat to low. Cover pan with a tight-fitting lid. Simmer rice 15 minutes. Remove from heat and let stand, undisturbed, 10 minutes. Fluff rice with a fork. Makes 3 cups.

ORIENTAL-STYLE LONG-GRAIN RICE

Long-grain rice is the table rice of China and most of Southeast Asia. It is cooked without salt or fat. Thailand's scented jasmine rice and Texas-grown Jasmati® have a very special aroma and flavor. To cook one cup of either rice, reduce the water amount suggested below by one-quarter cup. In Southeast Asia, rice is sometimes cooked with unsweetened coconut milk.

2 cups bottled spring water or tap water
1 cup long-grain rice, rinsed as directed on page 12

In a medium-size saucepan, combine water and rice; soak 30 minutes. Bring to a boil. Cover pan tightly; reduce heat to low. Simmer 15 minutes. Remove from heat; let stand, undisturbed, 10 minutes. Fluff rice with a large damp wooden spoon. Keep covered; remove as needed to a serving bowl. Makes about 3-1/2 cups.

Variation
To cook 2 cups rice, increase water to 3 cups.

SUSHI RICE

Use slightly less water to produce the characteristic chewy texture of sushi rice. The ample salt in the seasoning is necessary to create a delicate sweet-sour balance of flavors. Kokuho Rose and Kokusai Rose™ are premium strains of rice and "connoisseur's choices" for making sushi.

2 cups California medium- or short-grain rice, rinsed as directed on page 12
1 (3-inch) piece dried kelp (konbu)
2-1/3 cups bottled spring water or tap water

Awaze-Zu:
1/4 cup rice vinegar
2 tablespoons sugar
1 tablespoon mirin
1 tablespoon sake
1-1/2 teaspoons salt

Soak rice and kelp in the water 30 minutes. Cook as directed in the recipe for Cooked Medium-Grain Rice (page 17). Discard kelp just before water boils. Prepare Awaze-Zu. Scoop hot rice into an odorless, damp wooden bowl or glass bowl. Drizzle Awaze-Zu over rice and toss gently with a damp rice paddle or large damp wooden spoon. Fan rice to cool the grains and impart a shine. Add only as much dressing as the rice will absorb without becoming wet. Use at once or cover with a damp cloth. Do not refrigerate; rice will become hard. Use the same day. Makes about 5-1/2 cups.

Awaze-Zu
In a small saucepan over low heat, combine all ingredients. Makes 1/2 cup.

FRAGRANT BASMATI PILAF

This pilaf looks like plain cooked rice, but don't be fooled—each aromatic bite contains an explosion of flavor!

1 cup basmati or American-style basmati rice, rinsed as directed on page 12
2 tablespoons Ghee (page 21) or 1 tablespoon each vegetable oil and butter
1 small onion, cut in half, sliced paper-thin
1/4 teaspoon cumin seeds
3 whole green cardamom pods, slightly crushed
Pinch ground cinnamon
1 garlic clove, finely minced

In a medium-size bowl, cover rice with water; soak 30 minutes or until water is chalky. Drain well. Heat Ghee in a large skillet over medium-low heat. Add onion and spices; cook 5 minutes. Stir in garlic; cook 1 minute. Reduce heat to lowest setting. Bring 3-1/2 quarts salted water to a boil in a large saucepan. Add rice. When water boils, cook rice about 6 minutes, just until tender. American-style basmati takes about 12 minutes to cook. Drain rice well; add to onion mixture and stir 1 minute. Cover pan tightly; turn off heat. Let rice stand, undisturbed, 10 minutes. Fluff with a fork. Serve at once. Makes 3 or 4 servings.

Variations

Create a vegetarian main dish by stirring in 1-1/2 cups cooked lentils or beans.

To make plain rice, boil rice about 7 minutes; drain and place in a covered casserole dish. Place in a warm oven or warming drawer 15 minutes or until fluffy.

Microwave Basmati: Rice in the microwave works well, but there are generally no time savings. Julie Sahni, Indian cooking authority, states that basmati can be successfully microwaved in 12 to 16 minutes with no presoaking. She instructs cooks to place 1 cup rinsed basmati and 2-1/4 cups water in a microwave dish. Cook the rice, uncovered, at full power (HIGH) in a 650-watt carousel microwave oven 8 to 10 minutes or until the surface is covered with steam holes. Stir twice while cooking. Cover; cook at full power (HIGH) 4 to 6 minutes or until rice is soft. Let rice stand, covered, 5 minutes. Fluff with a fork.

Cooked Medium-Grain Rice

Japanese- and Korean- American cooks prefer sticky, medium-grain California rice,
which is perfect for eating with chopsticks. New crop rice for cooking.

1-1/2 cups bottled spring water or tap water
1 cup medium- or short-grain rice, rinsed as directed on page 12

In a medium-size saucepan, combine water and rice; soak 30 minutes. Bring to a boil. Cover pan tightly; reduce heat to low. Simmer 15 minutes. Remove from heat; let stand, undisturbed, 10 minutes. Fluff rice with a large damp wooden spoon. Keep covered; remove as needed to a serving bowl. Makes about 3 cups.

Variation
To cook 2 cups rice, increase water to 2-1/2 cups.

Cooked Whole-Wheat Berries

Cooked wheat berries lend a special chewiness to dishes to which they are added.
Mix them into other cooked grains, salads, bread doughs or serve with butter or sauce,
like rice. In the Middle East, wheat berries are cooked with dried beans and legumes or
simmered in sugar syrup with nuts, raisins and orange blossom water. Cooked wheat
berries can be prepared up to three days in advance and refrigerated until needed.

1 cup whole-wheat berries
About 3 cups water

Soak wheat berries in 3 cups water overnight. Simmer in soaking water over medium heat 1 hour, or to the desired degree of chewiness. Add additional water, if necessary. If wheat berries are to be added to bread dough, simmer only 25 minutes. Drain and cool before using. Makes about 2 cups.

SOAKED BULGUR

Bulgur can be soaked in hot water for a short period or cooked like rice. A cold water soak takes twice as long. Liquid amounts and cooking times vary, depending on the intended use of the bulgur and the degree of chewiness desired by the cook. Fine-milled bulgur requires less soaking and cooking time than a coarse grind. Soaked bulgur is good for salads like tabbouleh.

1 cup bulgur
3-1/2 cups boiling Homemade Chicken Stock (page 24), canned chicken broth or water
Salt (optional)

Place bulgur in a medium-size heatproof bowl; cover with boiling stock and salt, if using. Soak 45 minutes or longer to obtain the desired texture. Drain in a fine mesh sieve; press out excess water. Place bulgur in a medium-size bowl; fluff with a fork. Use as part of a recipe or serve with butter and minced herbs as a side dish. Makes 3 cups.

Variation

Simmered Bulgur: Place ingredients in a medium-size saucepan over low heat; cover tightly. Simmer 25 minutes or until water is absorbed. If the grains are still too chewy, add a little more boiling water; cook until absorbed. Remove from heat; let stand, undisturbed, 10 minutes.

Cooked Barley

Barley is an ancient grain which is often mentioned in the Bible. It is a nutritious alternative to rice. Serve it as a side dish, a salad, add it to breads or combine with other cooked grains. Soak barley to cut the cooking time in half.

About 3-1/2 to 4 cups homemade stock (page 24), canned chicken broth or water
1/2 teaspoon salt, or to taste
1 cup pearl barley
Butter to taste

Bring 3-1/2 cups broth and salt to a boil in a 3-quart pot. Add barley. Cover pan; simmer 35 to 40 minutes or until tender. If barley is not tender and stock has evaporated, add additional stock. Fluff cooked barley with a fork. Serve as a side dish with butter or use in recipes. Makes 3 cups.

Cooked Quinoa

Quinoa is a quick-cooking nutritional "supergrain" which tastes delicious and has an interesting texture and appearance. When cooked, the tiny seeds become translucent and moist. Serve quinoa as you would rice, with butter and seasonings. Or, mix a portion into cooked rice or other grains. Remember to rinse quinoa well to remove any possible bitter taste.

1 cup quinoa
2 cups Homemade Chicken Stock (page 24), canned chicken broth or water

In a large bowl, cover quinoa with cool water. Rinse well; drain in a fine mesh sieve. Place quinoa in a medium-size, heavy saucepan. Toast over medium-high heat 4 to 5 minutes, shaking pan or stirring constantly, until quinoa dries and just begins to pop. The color will change slightly, but do not allow quinoa to darken. Pour in stock. Bring to a boil. Reduce heat to low; cover with a tight-fitting lid. Cook 15 minutes or until the grains become tender and fairly dry. Season and serve as a side dish or use in recipes. Makes about 3 cups.

TOASTED NUTS, SEEDS & GRAINS

The flavor of nuts, seeds and grains is greatly enhanced by toasting.

Whole nuts, seeds or grains

Spread nuts on a heavy baking sheet or 2 thin baking sheets stacked to insulate against burning. Preheat oven to 300°F (150°C). Place in oven and toast 5 minutes or until nuts are fragrant and lightly browned. Watch carefully to prevent burning.

Toast sesame seeds or wheat germ in a small, dry heavy skillet over medium-high heat, until aromatic and golden-brown. Shake pan constantly. To release the fragrant oils, use a pestle to bruise the seeds in a mortar. For maximum freshness, toast seeds as you need them. To toast grains such as millet or quinoa, put them into a heavy skillet over medium-high heat; cook, stirring, 3 to 5 minutes, until fragrant and light golden-brown. Watch carefully to prevent scorching. Barley, buckwheat groats and oats can be toasted on a baking sheet in a 350°F (175°C) oven 10 minutes, until golden-brown. Stir several times.

Variation
Dried spices can be toasted as above, then ground in an electric spice grinder.

POPPED AMARANTH

When popped, tiny amaranth seeds resemble miniature kernels of white popped corn. Mix popped amaranth into salad dressings, cereals, cookie doughs, or use as a crunchy garnish.

Amaranth seeds

Heat a 10- to 12-inch heavy skillet over medium-high heat. Add 1/2 tablespoon seeds to the hot pan. Immediately cover pan. Amaranth should pop within 5 seconds. Shake pan constantly 10 to 15 seconds while the seeds pop. A few seeds will remain unpopped. Pour into a dish to cool; use as desired.

Note
Do not pop more than the recommended amount of seeds at once; larger amounts do not pop efficiently.

GHEE

In an Indian kitchen, this pure butterfat is worth its weight in gold. Ghee won't burn like ordinary butter and imparts a rich nutty flavor. Ghee is similar to clarified butter except it is simmered over low heat until the milk solids at the bottom of the pot turn golden-brown. For flavor variety in cooking, Indian cooks simmer Ghee with gingerroot, spices or chiles.

2 pounds top-quality unsalted butter (no substitute)

In a heavy, medium-size saucepan, melt butter over very low heat. The milk protein will separate and sink to the bottom. Cook 1 hour or until the milk solids turn light golden-brown. Watch carefully; do not allow milk solids to become any darker. Cool slightly; pour into a large bowl through a fine mesh strainer lined with several layers of cheese-cloth. Store in a tightly covered jar in the refrigerator up to about 3 months. Makes about 2-3/4 cups.

Soups

Barley, quinoa, amaranth, kasha and millet. These exotic names read like a rogue's galley of grains! You know they are good for you, but how will you convince your family, especially the kids, of their value? One delicious way to incorporate more of these grains into your diet is to add them to homemade soups. The base of any richly flavored soup or stew is always a good stock such as the Homemade Chicken Stock or Homemade Beef Stock (page 24). If you prefer, use a vegetable stock or water and vegetable juices.

To prepare a simple, nourishing soup, begin with the stock and simmer it with a few aromatic vegetables and a handful of wholesome grains. Grains act as a natural thickener. Flours made of grains such as rice and barley have a delicate taste and can also be used to thicken soups. Mexican Posole & Black Bean Stew (page 33) can be slightly thickened by stirring in a small amount of either fine cornmeal or masa harina, a Mexican corn flour used for making tortillas.

To complete your homemade soup, toss in some favorite herbs or spices to round out the flavor. Herbs and spices are at their best when added to soups. Their distinctive tastes permeate the warm savory liquid, adding character through flavor and color. What could be more delicious on a cold day than a hearty bowl of Cracked Wheat Soup with Spiced Turkey Meatballs (page 31), perfumed with fresh mint and cilantro?

Many soups can be prepared a day in advance; gentle reheating enhances the flavors. Beef & Barley Soup with Shiitake Mushrooms (page 26) is a soup I always make a day or two ahead to allow the flavors plenty of time to blend.

Cajun Catfish & Okra Gumbo (page 27) is a hearty stew which is ready to serve in about 45 minutes. The complex, spicy flavors of the gumbo become mellow when blended into bowls of soothing plain white rice.

Mushroom & Wild Rice Chowder (page 30) is a filling soup which can also be made with barley or buckweat.

HOMEMADE CHICKEN STOCK

A pot of soup is only as flavorful as the stock which goes into it. Do not salt the stock; it will become too salty when it is reduced. Make a bouquet garni by tying fresh herbs together with kitchen string. I suggest using two sprigs each of parsley and thyme and one bay leaf.

5 pounds uncooked mixed chicken parts and bones
1 large onion, cut into large pieces
1 leafy celery stalk, cut into pieces
1 medium-size carrot, cut into pieces
5 peppercorns
1 bouquet garni
About 4 quarts water

In a stockpot, bring all the ingredients to a boil. Skim off foam which forms on top. Reduce heat to low; simmer, uncovered, at least 4 hours. If necessary, replenish water level to maintain 3 quarts of stock in the pot. For a richer, more concentrated flavor, reduce stock to 2 quarts. Strain stock; discard solids. For greater clarity, strain stock in a fine strainer lined with cheesecloth. Cool and refrigerate. Skim off fat; use within 3 days or freeze in 1-quart amounts. Makes about 3 quarts.

Variations

Homemade Beef Stock: Omit chicken parts; substitute 5 pounds beef shanks. Roast in a 450°F (230°C) oven 40 minutes. Add vegetables; roast 20 minutes and add to stockpot with seasonings, 1 chopped tomato and 1 garlic clove. Continue as directed above.

Chicken Stock with Ginger: To make stock suitable for Asian dishes, prepare Homemade Chicken Stock, above. Omit celery, carrot and bouquet garni; add 4 (1/4-inch-thick) diagonal slices of fresh gingerroot. Continue as directed above.

Enriched Canned Broth: If you are short on time and need stock in a hurry, you can vastly improve the flavor of canned chicken broth. Simmer 5 cups of canned broth (about 45 oz.) with 1 pound of chicken parts, 2 sliced green onions, 5 peppercorns and a bouquet garni. Simmer 30 minutes; strain and use.

CREAMY TOMATO & TORTILLA SOUP

Crunchy fried corn tortilla strips lend texture and a rich corn taste to this colorful tomato soup. The tortilla strips fry much better if they are dried at room temperature for several hours.

1 tablespoon olive oil
1/2 red bell pepper, chopped
2 green onions, chopped
2 garlic cloves, chopped
1/2 teaspoon cumin seeds
1/2 teaspoon ground cumin
4 cups Homemade Chicken Stock (page 24) or canned chicken broth
2 cups chopped, peeled tomatoes
1/4 cup sun-dried tomato paste or regular tomato paste
2 teaspoons sugar
1/2 teaspoon salt, or to taste
1 jalapeño or serrano chile (optional), seeded and minced
1 rounded tablespoon white cornmeal
4 corn tortillas, cut into thin 1/8-inch strips and deep-fried until crisp
1/4 cup grated queso añejo, Parmigiano or Romano cheese
Fresh cilantro leaves

In a large saucepan, heat oil over medium heat. Add bell pepper, onions, garlic, cumin seeds and ground cumin; sauté 1 minute. Add stock and tomatoes. Whisk in tomato paste, sugar, salt and chile, if using. Simmer, partially covered, 10 minutes on low heat. Stir in cornmeal. Pour soup into the bowl of a food processor fitted with the steel blade. Puree until smooth. Pour back into the pot. Simmer 4 minutes over low heat. Crush tortilla strips into halves. Ladle soup into shallow bowls. Scatter tortilla strips, cheese and cilantro leaves on each serving. Makes 4 servings.

Variation
Omit tortilla strips and stir in about 1/2 cup of a cooked nutritional supergrain such as millet, amaranth or quinoa.

Beef & Barley Soup with Shiitake Mushrooms

Barley adds a pleasant, chewy texture and a wholesome goodness to this hearty soup.

2 tablespoons olive oil
1-1/4 to 1-1/2 pounds beef chuck roast, fat trimmed
1 medium-size onion, chopped
2 celery stalks, diced
2 garlic cloves, minced
4 cups Homemade Beef Stock (page 24) or canned beef broth
4 cups water
1 cup crushed tomatoes
2 medium-size dried shiitake mushrooms or 1/4 pound sliced button mushrooms
1 tablespoon soy sauce
1 teaspoon dried leaf thyme
1/2 cup fine, pearled barley
1 large carrot, diced
Salt and ground pepper to taste
Hot sauce to taste

Heat oil in a large pot. Add beef and sauté on all sides until browned. Add onion, celery and garlic; cook 1 minute. Add the stock, tomatoes, mushrooms, soy sauce and thyme. Partially cover pan; simmer 1 hour. Add barley and carrot. Cook 1 hour or until beef and barley are tender. Remove beef and mushrooms. Cut beef into soup-size chunks. Discard mushroom stems; dice mushroom caps. Add beef and mushrooms back to the pot. Add salt, pepper and hot sauce. Makes 6 servings.

Variation
Substitute grian sorghum that has been soaked in water overnight for pearled barley. Add sorghum 30 minutes before soup is done.

Cajun Catfish & Okra Gumbo

To reduce fat in this spicy gumbo, I use a flavor base of nutty-tasting browned flour instead of the traditional flour and fat roux. When browned, the flour loses some thickening power, but the okra also acts as a thickener.

1/3 cup all-purpose flour, sifted
3 tablespoons olive oil
1 cup chopped onion
1 cup finely chopped red or green bell pepper
1 celery stalk, diced
2 garlic cloves, minced
2 cups sliced fresh okra or 1 (10-oz.) box frozen sliced okra, thawed
4 cups Homemade Chicken Stock (page 24) or canned chicken broth
1 cup peeled, chopped tomatoes
1/4 teaspoon ground black pepper
3/4 teaspoon dried leaf thyme
1 tablespoon minced fresh parsley
1 recipe Cooked Long-Grain Rice (page 14)
3/4 to 1 pound fresh catfish fillets, cut into small cubes
2 green onions, finely minced
Hot pepper sauce to taste

Place flour into a small heavy skillet over medium-low heat. Cook 25 minutes, stirring often, or until flour is aromatic and turns medium-brown. Do not allow flour to burn. Set aside. Heat oil in a 3-quart saucepan over medium heat. Add onion, bell pepper, celery and garlic; cook until soft. Add okra; cook 3 minutes more. Stir in 3 tablespoons browned flour. Add stock, tomato, black pepper, thyme and parsley. Bring to a boil; reduce heat and simmer 30 minutes. Prepare rice. Add catfish and green onions to gumbo. Cook 10 minutes or until fish begins to flake. Place 1/2 cup rice into each of 4 or 5 deep soup bowls; fill with gumbo. Makes 4 or 5 servings.

Country Garden Vegetable Soup with Buckwheat Groats

This nutritious, garden-fresh soup can be ready to serve in about one hour. Buckwheat groats are whole, hulled buckwheat seeds. Unlike roasted buckwheat groats or kasha, the white groats have a delicate, mild taste. Buckwheat has more usable protein than most grains, and contains a high proportion of all eight essential amino acids, including lysine.

3 tablespoons olive oil
1 large red onion, chopped
1 small red or green bell pepper, diced
1 carrot, thinly sliced
1 celery stalk, thinly sliced
8 ounces lean beef, fat trimmed, cut into 1/2-inch cubes
2 garlic cloves, minced
1-1/2 pounds tomatoes, peeled, seeded, chopped or 1 (28-oz.) can Italian plum
    tomatoes with liquid, chopped
1 (6-oz.) can tomato paste
5 cups Homemade Beef Stock (page 24) or canned beef broth
2 tablespoons each chopped fresh parsley and thyme
1 teaspoon sugar
1/4 teaspoon freshly grated nutmeg
1/2 cup whole white buckwheat groats
Salt and freshly ground black pepper to taste

Heat 1 tablespoon of the oil in a large pot over medium-high heat. When hot, add onion, bell pepper, carrot and celery; sauté 1 minute. Remove vegetables to a platter. Reheat pan with remaining oil. Add meat and sauté until browned. Add garlic, reserved vegetables, tomatoes, tomato paste and stock. Stir in herbs, sugar and nutmeg. Bring to a boil; reduce heat to low. Cover and simmer 20 minutes. Add buckwheat groats; simmer 20 minutes or until beef and buckwheat are tender. Add salt and black pepper. Serve hot. Makes 6 servings.

CREAMY ALMOND SOUP WITH SAFFRON

This delicate soup is perfumed with almond and saffron. Tender short-grain Italian rice is especially nice in this soup because the grains cook quickly but do not become mushy. Or, use any other flavorful short- or medium-grain rice.

1 cup whipping cream
1/4 teaspoon crushed saffron threads
2 tablespoons butter or margarine
3 shallots, thinly sliced
1 cup toasted, slivered almonds
About 3 cups Homemade Chicken Stock (page 24) or canned chicken broth
2 tablespoons cornstarch mixed with 2 tablespoons cold water
1 cup cooked medium- or short-grain rice
1/2 poached chicken breast, skinned, boned, diced
Salt and ground white pepper to taste
1/4 cup sliced toasted almonds
1 tablespoon snipped fresh chives

Pour cream into a small bowl; stir in saffron. In a medium-size saucepan, melt butter over medium heat. Add shallots and almonds; cook, stirring constantly, until golden-brown. Remove from heat. In a blender or food processor fitted with the steel blade, process almond mixture to a paste consistency. Scrape mixture back into saucepan. Add 3 cups stock. Reduce heat to low. Cover pan; simmer 20 minutes. Press hot stock through a fine mesh strainer into a medium-size bowl; discard almond pulp. Measure 2-1/2 cups; if necessary, add more stock. Rinse saucepan; pour in stock. Heat over medium-high heat. Stir in cornstarch mixture; cook until thickened. Reduce heat. Stir in saffron-cream, rice, chicken, salt and pepper. Garnish each serving with almonds and chives. Makes 4 or 5 servings.

MUSHROOM & WILD RICE CHOWDER

Serve this hearty chowder for lunch or supper with crusty rolls and a salad.

1/4 cup unsalted butter or margarine
2 small green onions, minced
1 garlic clove, minced
2 cups sliced medium-size button mushrooms
1/2 cup chopped green bell pepper
1 celery stalk, chopped
3 tablespoons all-purpose flour
2 cups Homemade Chicken Stock (page 24) or canned chicken broth
1/2 cup whipping cream
2 tablespoons chopped pimento
Salt and black pepper to taste
1 cup cooked wild rice
2 tablespoons dry sherry

Melt butter in a medium-size saucepan over medium heat. Add onions and garlic; sauté 30 seconds. Add mushrooms, bell pepper and celery; cook 5 minutes. In a medium-size bowl, blend flour with stock; stir into saucepan. Simmer 6 to 8 minutes or until thickened. Stir in cream, pimento, salt and black pepper. Simmer 2 to 3 minutes. Stir in wild rice and sherry. Serve hot. Makes 3 servings.

CRACKED WHEAT SOUP WITH SPICED TURKEY MEATBALLS

Cracked wheat is made from whole-wheat berries. Often used in Middle Eastern cooking, it is delicious simmered in soups.

6 cups Homemade Chicken Stock (page 24) or canned chicken broth
1/2 cup cracked wheat
1/2 pound lean ground turkey
1/2 to 1 small fresh green chile, minced
2 tablespoons minced onion
1 garlic clove, minced
1/8 teaspoon each ground cinnamon and ground cumin
2 small green onions, minced
2 tablespoons each minced fresh mint and cilantro
1/4 teaspoon each salt and pepper

In a large pot, bring stock and cracked wheat to a boil. Reduce heat, cover and simmer 20 minutes or until tender. Prepare meatballs by combining turkey with chile, onion, garlic and spices in a medium-size bowl. Use 1 tablespoon meat mixture for each meatball. Drop meatballs into soup; poach until they float to the top and are cooked through. Stir in green onions, herbs, salt and pepper. Serve hot. Makes 4 or 5 servings.

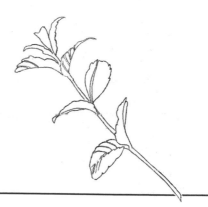

LEMON-CHICKEN SOUP
WITH SEMOLINA-PARMESAN DUMPLINGS

The tender dumplings are made of semolina and Parmesan cheese with a hint of fresh lemon.
Do not poach the dumplings too long or at too high a temperature or they will toughen.

Semolinea-Parmesan Dumpings, see below
5 cups Homemade Chicken Stock (page 24) or canned chicken broth
2 tablespoons fresh lemon juice
About 3/4 cup tightly packed, shredded fresh spinach leaves
2 teaspoons shredded fresh sage leaves
Salt and pepper to taste

Semolina-Parmesan Dumplings:
2 tablespoons butter or margarine
1/3 cup semolina
1/3 cup grated Parmesan cheese
1/2 teaspoon freshly grated lemon peel
Pinch of freshly grated nutmeg
1/8 teaspoon salt
2 large eggs
4 or 5 cups water
4 or 5 chicken bouillon granules

Prepare dumplings. Heat stock and lemon juice in a large saucepan over medium-low heat. Simmer until hot. Add spinach, sage, salt and pepper. Add poached dumplings; simmer 1 minute. Ladle soup and dumplings into shallow serving bowls. Makes 4 servings.

Semolina-Parmesan Dumplings
In a medium-size saucepan, melt butter; stir in semolina, cheese, lemon peel, nutmeg and salt. Beat in eggs, one at time, until smooth. Spread mixture in an 8-inch-square pan. Refrigerate 2 hours or overnight. In a medium-size saucepan, combine water with bouillon granules; bring to a simmer, stirring to dissolve granules. Push rounded teaspoons of the dumpling mixture into the simmering liquid. Do not stir. Cook 2 to 3 minutes or until dumplings float. Remove from broth with a slotted spoon. Add to soup. Makes about 20 dumplings.

Mexican Posole & Black Bean Stew

In Mexico, posole, or hominy, is often added to meat stews. Make this dish a day ahead; overnight refrigeration will enhance the flavors. If you prefer a thicker stew, stir in one to two tablespoons masa, a special cornmeal made from ground hominy.

1 tablespoon olive oil
1 medium-size onion, chopped
1 celery stalk, chopped
1 small green bell pepper
2 garlic cloves, minced
1/2 pound lean pork sausage
1/2 pound lean ground turkey
1 heaping teaspoon each ground cumin, dried leaf oregano and paprika
1-1/2 to 2 tablespoons ground dried chiles
2 cups Homemade Chicken Stock (page 24) or canned chicken broth
1/4 cup sun-dried tomato paste or regular tomato paste
1 (10-oz.) can diced tomatoes and green chiles
1 (15-oz.) can golden hominy, drained
1 (15-oz.) can black beans, rinsed, drained
1/3 cup sliced ripe olives
2 tablespoons minced fresh cilantro
1 teaspoon salt, or to taste
Crushed corn chips

Heat oil in medium-size pot. Add onion, celery, bell pepper and garlic; sauté 3 minutes. Add sausage, turkey, cumin, oregano, paprika and chili powder; cook, stirring to break up meat, until no longer pink. Add stock, tomato paste, tomatoes and chiles and hominy. Cover and simmer 20 minutes. Add black beans, olives, cilantro and salt; cook 15 minutes. Sprinkle crushed corn chips on top of each serving. Makes 4 servings.

Salads

Salad once meant a bowlful of that faithful old standby—iceberg lettuce tossed with the standard formula of sliced radishes, cucumbers and tomatoes. Today, we are adventurously blending whole grains, vegetables and herbs to create a new genre of salads. Familiar whole grains and the less familiar "new grains" such as quinoa and amaranth are adding an exciting and creative new dimension to the concept of saladmaking.

Composed salads were often extraordinary works of art during the Elizabethan period. "Sallets," as they were known, were seasoned with herbs, oil, vinegar and black pepper. The Garden Tomatoes Stuffed with Marinated Quinoa (page 39) are no less extraordinary when arranged on pretty serving plates lined with tender, young lettuce leaves. Quinoa, a South American grain, not only tastes good, but is nutritionally superior to most other grains.

Compose your salads with thought and care to create a balance of flavors, colors and textures. Use only the finest seasonal ingredients. To create grain salads with panache, toss them with distinctive-flavored herbs such as dill, basil and mint that will lend variety in taste and character. Corn Bread Salad with Parsley-Chive Dressing (page 43) is an unusual but appetizing salad, featuring chunks of freshly made cornbread, garden vegetables and crisp bacon dressed with a flavorful herb mayonnaise.

Experiment with distinctive-tasting greens such as magenta-colored baby radicchio leaves, arugula, chicory, sorrel, fernlike mizuna or colorful edible flowers. Frisée (curly endive), mâche (lamb's lettuce), purslane, Japanese shungiku, carrot tops or shepherd's purse can also be used to decorate plates and garnish whole-grain salads.

Edible containers are great fun and can be fashioned from hollowed fruits and vegetables, cabbage cups or fried flour tortilla shells. Or, stuff your grain salads into Whole-Wheat-Pocket Breads (page 82) as suggested in the recipe for Fresh Mint, Parsley & Dill Tabbouleh (page 38).

CURRIED KAMUT
& GARDEN VEGETABLE MEDLEY

Kamut is an ancient wheat with a mild, buttery taste and a delicate, chewy texture. It resembles large grains of brown rice. For an extraordinary grain salad, try this recipe with half kamut and half cooked sweet Wehani®, a marvelous brown rice blend of California basmati, sweet dessert rice, russet Wehani and long-grain rice.

4 cups water
1 cup uncooked kamut
1/2 cup top-quality mayonnaise or low-calorie mayonnaise
1/4 cup plain yogurt
1 garlic clove, finely minced
1/2 teaspoon curry powder
1/4 teaspoon turmeric
2 cups small broccoli flowerets, blanched 1 minute, chilled in iced water, drained
1 cup diced carrots, blanched 30 seconds, chilled in iced water, drained
1 red bell pepper, finely diced
3 small green onions, thinly sliced
2 tablespoons dried currants
1/4 cup minced fresh parsley
2 lemons, cut into wedges

In a medium-size saucepan, bring water and kamut to a boil. Reduce heat; cover and simmer 1-1/2 hours or until tender. Cool kamut. Place into a large bowl; blend with mayonnaise, yogurt, garlic, curry powder and turmeric. Toss in remaining ingredients except lemon wedges. Garnish with lemon wedges. Makes 4 to 6 servings.

MEDITERRANEAN RICE & SEAFOOD SALAD

Fresh seafood, tangy lemon and fragrant herbs give plain rice a special cadence. Serve this salad at room temperature on a lettuce-lined platter. If made one or two hours ahead, stir in the chilled seafood at the last minute.

1/3 cup extra-virgin olive oil
3 tablespoons fresh lemon juice
Freshly grated peel of 1 lemon
2 tablespoons minced fresh tarragon or dill or 2 teaspoons dried leaf tarragon or dill
1 garlic clove, finely minced
Salt and pepper to taste
1 recipe Cooked Long-Grain Rice (page 14)
1 pound mixed cooked seafood (shrimp, crab, lobster, smoked mussels, flaked salmon)
1/2 cup chopped celery
1/3 cup thinly sliced small green onions
1/4 cup minced fresh Italian parsley
2 tablespoons minced Kalamata olives
1 tablespoon capers
Lettuce leaves
1/4 cup toasted pine nuts

In a medium-size bowl, whisk together olive oil, lemon juice, lemon peel, tarragon, garlic, salt and pepper; set aside. Prepare rice and let cool. In a large bowl, toss rice with seafood, celery, green onions, parsley, olives and capers. Blend in dressing. Line a serving bowl with lettuce leaves; spoon salad into bowl. Garnish with pine nuts. Makes 4 to 6 servings.

Fresh Mint, Parsley & Dill Tabbouleh

Serve this Middle Eastern favorite on a bed of romaine lettuce with slices of fresh tomatoes. Or, spoon the tabbouleh into hollowed-out red and yellow tomatoes. For an appealing variation, make this dish with Riz Cous, broken grains of brown rice which resemble couscous.

1 recipe Soaked Bulgur (page 18)
2 green onions, minced
1/4 cup minced fresh parsley
2 tablespoons minced fresh dill
2 tablespoons minced fresh mint
3 tablespoons extra-virgin olive oil
3 tablespoons fresh lemon juice
1 teaspoon salt
1 garlic clove, minced

Prepare Soaked Bulgur and place into a large bowl. Stir in green onions and herbs. In a small bowl, whisk together olive oil, lemon juice, salt and garlic. Pour over bulgur; toss to combine. Serve at once, or cover tightly and refrigerate up to 2 days. Makes 4 servings.

Garden Tomatoes Stuffed with Marinated Quinoa

Quinoa, the "mother of all grains," was an important food for the ancient Incas and has survived for thousands of years, thriving under the most severe ecological conditions.

1/2 recipe Cooked Quinoa (page 19)
2 tablespoons balsamic vinegar
1 to 2 tablespoons extra-virgin olive oil
Salt and pepper to taste
1 garlic clove, finely minced
2 tablespoons minced fresh parsley
1 green onion, finely minced
1 tablespoon finely minced green olives
4 medium-size tomatoes, peeled, centers scooped out
Leaf lettuce

Prepare quinoa. When cool, place in a medium-size bowl with all the remaining ingredients except tomatoes and lettuce. Spoon quinoa mixture into tomato shells. Line 4 plates with lettuce, and place each stuffed tomato on a plate. Makes 4 servings.

Note
An easy way to peel the tomatoes is to drop them in boiling water 30 seconds, then submerge them briefly in iced water. The skins will peel off easily after this process.

TURKISH EGGPLANT & QUINOA SALAD

Roast the eggplant on an outdoor grill to intensify its flavor. For a great sandwich, stuff a portion of the eggplant and quinoa mixture, sliced tomatoes, lettuce and sprouts into Whole-Wheat Pocket Breads (page 81).

1 (1-lb.) eggplant or 4 (4-oz.) purple Oriental eggplants, pierced with a fork
1 cup Cooked Quinoa (page 19)
1/4 cup minced fresh parsley
3 small green onions, finely minced
2 garlic cloves, finely minced
3 tablespoons fresh lemon juice
2 tablespoons extra-virgin olive oil
1 tablespoon toasted sesame seeds (page 20), crushed
Salt and pepper to taste
Fresh leaf lettuce
1/3 cup toasted pine nuts or coarsely chopped walnuts
Lemon wedges
4 Whole-Wheat Pocket Breads (page 82), toasted, cut into wedges

Preheat oven to 425°F (220°C). Place eggplant on a heavy baking sheet; roast 30 minutes or until the skin blackens and the pulp is soft. If using small eggplants, roast 20 minutes. Prepare quinoa. Allow eggplant to cool; peel off skin. Chop finely with a large knife or in the food processor using the metal blade. Place pulp into a large bowl; stir in quinoa, parsley, onions, garlic, lemon juice, olive oil, sesame seeds, salt and pepper. Line a serving platter with lettuce leaves. Spoon salad onto platter; garnish with pine nuts and lemon wedges. Serve with pocket breads. Makes 4 or 5 servings.

Barley, Green Bean & Olive Summer Salad

Barley is a delicious, naturally sweet-tasting grain. A cup of cooked pearl barley provides the same amount of protein as a glass of milk. The green beans are microwaved to preserve their bright color, fresh flavor and valuable nutrients. You will enjoy serving this colorful salad year round.

---

1 recipe Cooked Barley (page 19)
1-1/4 pounds small fresh green beans
1/4 cup pitted and coarsely chopped Kalamata or other brine-cured olives
2 tablespoons coarsely chopped walnuts
Musttard Vinaigrette, see below
4 slices crisp-cooked bacon, crumbled

Mustard Vinaigrette:
1/4 cup extra-virgin olive oil
3 tablespoons red-wine vinegar
1 tablespoon minced fresh basil or 1 teaspoon dried leaf basil
1 shallot, finely minced
1 garlic clove, finely minced
2 teaspoons whole-grain mustard
1/2 teaspoon sugar
1/4 teaspoon salt, or to taste

Prepare barley. Spread half of the beans on an ovenproof plate; sprinkle with water. Cover with plastic wrap. Microwave on full power (HIGH) 4 to 5 minutes. Allow covered beans to stand, undisturbed, 5 minutes. Cook remaining beans. When cool, cut beans into 1-inch pieces. In a large bowl, toss barley, beans, olives and walnuts. Prepare Mustard Vinaigrette. Toss with barley salad. Garnish each serving with bacon. Makes 4 or 5 servings.

Mustard Vinaigrette
In a small bowl, whisk together all ingredients. Makes about 1/2 cup.

Buckwheat, Lentil & Sausage Salad

Buckwheat reigns as a top source of plant protein, coming close to the composition of animal protein. Precook the whole groats in egg white to keep them separate and fluffy after cooking. The flavors in this robust salad are at their peak when served at room temperature.

1 cup buckwheat groats
1 large egg white
2 cups Homemade Chicken Stock (page 24), canned chicken broth or water
1/2 cup lentils, rinsed
1 medium-size red bell pepper, roasted, peeled, diced
1 (6- to 8-inch) piece low-fat turkey kielbasa, thinly sliced
1/2 cup thinly sliced celery
1/4 cup chopped pitted oil-cured ripe olives
3 small green onions, thinly sliced
Herb Vinaigrette, see below
Romaine lettuce leaves

Herb Vinaigrette:
1/2 cup extra-virgin olive oil
1/3 cup red-wine vinegar
2 garlic cloves, finely minced
1 tablespoon each minced fresh parsley and basil or oregano
1/2 teaspoon salt, or to taste
Pepper to taste

Mix buckwheat and egg white in a medium-size skillet. Place over medium-high heat; stir 3 to 4 minutes or until the groats are dry. Turn off heat; slowly stir in stock with a long wooden spoon. Cover pan. Simmer over low heat 20 minutes or until groats are tender. Remove from heat. Allow groats to stand, undisturbed, 5 minutes. Cool completely. Simmer lentils in a large pot of salted boiling water 20 minutes or just until tender. Drain well; cool. In a large bowl, toss buckwheat groats, lentils and remaining ingredients except lettuce leaves. Prepare dressing; mix into salad ingredients. Arrange salad on a lettuce-lined platter; serve at once. Makes 5 or 6 servings.

Herb Vinaigrette
In a medium-size bowl, whisk together all ingredients. Makes about 1 cup.

CORN BREAD SALAD
WITH PARSLEY-CHIVE DRESSING

In the Middle East, salads are made with pita bread; in Tuscany, they are made with crusty Italian bread. In the South, we offer a real "down-home" version made with buttermilk corn bread. If you are one of those people who loves to nibble on cornbread dressing, you will appreciate this recipe!

1 recipe Lacy Cornmeal Cakes (page 91), prepared as directed below
2 celery stalks, chopped
8 to 10 red cherry tomatoes, cut in half
2 pickled okra, thinly sliced
1 small zucchini, halved lengthwise, sliced into 1/4-inch pieces
1 small green bell pepper, chopped
1/2 small red onion, thinly sliced, cut into quarters
Parsley-Chive Dressing, see below
4 or 5 slices crisp-cooked bacon, crumbled
2 ounces basil- and tomato-flavored feta cheese or plain feta cheese

Parsley-Chive Dressing:
1/2 cup top-quality regular mayonnaise or low-calorie mayonnaise
1 tablespoon red-wine vinegar
1 teaspoon sugar
1 heaping tablespoon each minced fresh parsley and chives
Salt and pepper to taste

Preheat oven to 375°F (190°C). Prepare cornmeal cake batter, adding only 2 tablespoons oil. Heat remaining 1/2 tablespoon oil in a 9- or 10-inch cast-iron skillet. Add batter; bake 15 minutes or until the bottom is crisp and golden-brown. Cool; place in a large bowl; break into chunks. Add vegetables to bowl. Prepare Parsley-Chive Dressing; spoon over salad. Gently mix ingredients. Spoon into a serving bowl; sprinkle with bacon and cheese. Serve at once or cover and refrigerate up to 2 hours. Makes 5 or 6 servings.

Parsley-Chive Dressing
In a small bowl, combine all ingredients. Makes about 1/2 cup.

Meat, Poultry & Seafood Entrees

For centuries, grains have been the mainstay in the diets of most civilizations. In our own society, we once considered these starchy carbohydrate foods to be too fattening to eat in large amounts, and believed the better way was to have more meat. Enlightened nutritional researchers have discovered the true path to good health is to eat less meat and to increase the complex-carbohydrate, whole-grain foods on our plates.

Grain cooking offers unlimited opportunities for creating nutritious, healthful main dishes. Eating more whole-grain foods will get us back to the basics of good nutrition and can replace a portion of the meat and processed, highly refined foods in our diets.

To decrease saturated fats and cholesterol in your diet, look east for culinary inspiration! In China, one-half pound of meat can be stretched to feed four or more people satisfactorily. Animal proteins are used sparingly, almost as a seasoning or condiment, to enhance the bulk of the meal which consists of vegetables and grains or grain foods. Rice, an incomplete protein, is often paired with a small portion of protein-rich meat, poultry, seafood or tofu, which has been dubbed "the meat of the fields." Together, they supply all the essential amino acids needed for good health. In the Japanese recipe Buckwheat Noodles with Crab Fritters (page 47) only four ounces of crabmeat are used to prepare this tasty meal for four people. The succulent dish Korean Rice Bowl with Spicy Beef (page 48) calls for less than three ounces of animal protein per person.

Couscous, a North African grainlike food made from semolina wheat, and bulgur are both eaten in the Middle East. Couscous is a delicious side dish with meat and poultry. Spice-Scented Couscous with Saffron Chicken (page 50) offers an easy approach to preparing couscous, which is usually steamed repeatedly in a somewhat time-consuming process. If you enjoy your initial taste, I encourage you to delve into the world of Middle Eastern cooking and master the traditional approach for preparing this versatile grain.

GINGER-BEEF & BARLEY STIR-FRY

Barley is a nutritious cereal grass, which can be prepared like fried rice. Rich in cholesterol-lowering dietary fiber, barley can be conveniently cooked in the microwave in half the traditional cooking time. It will expand in size three to four times the original amount. For this recipe, cook the barley several hours in advance.

1/2 cup fine pearl barley
3-1/2 cups water, heated to boiling
1/2 pound beef sirloin, thinly sliced, cut into 1-inch pieces
2 tablespoons soy sauce
1 tablespoon dry white wine
1/2 teaspoon cornstarch
1-1/2 teaspoons minced fresh gingerroot
3 tablespoons vegetable oil
2 small green onions, thinly sliced
1 large garlic clove, minced
1 celery stalk, thinly sliced
1/4 cup minced red bell pepper
1-1/2 cups sliced, medium-size button mushrooms
Salt and black pepper to taste

Place barley in a casserole dish; add 3-1/2 cups boiling water. Cover with vented plastic wrap. Microwave on full power (HIGH) 3 minutes. Reduce power to 50% (MEDIUM); cook 30 minutes longer. Let barley stand, covered, until cool. In a medium-size bowl, marinate beef in soy sauce, wine, cornstarch and gingerroot. Heat half the oil in a wok or large skillet over medium-high heat. Drain beef; stir-fry 1 minute or until no longer pink. Remove to a platter. Wipe pan dry. Reheat wok with remaining oil. Stir-fry onions, garlic, celery and bell pepper 1 minute. Add mushrooms; stir-fry 2 to 3 minutes. Reduce heat slightly. Stir in barley, then the beef with any juices. Season with salt and black pepper. When the barley is hot, scoop the mixture onto the platter. Makes 2 or 3 servings.

BUCKWHEAT NOODLES WITH CRAB FRITTERS

Japanese buckwheat noodles, or soba, began as an exclusive food for the temple priests. Combined with egg, seafood or meat, soba is a nutritious meal. Cooked soba has twice as much vitamin B_1 as cooked white rice.

4 cups Japanese fish stock (dashi) or Chicken Stock with Ginger (page 24)
1 teaspoon salt
3 tablespoons soy sauce
1 tablespoon sugar
1 tablespoon mirin
Crab Fitters, see below
1 pound dried Japanese soba noodles, cooked until al dente
12 spinach leaves, blanched 10 seconds, cut into pieces
2 green onions, minced

Crab Fitters:
1/2 cup cake flour
2 tablespoons cornstarch
1/4 teaspoon baking powder
1 small egg white
3/4 cup ice-cold sparkling water, more if needed
2 green onions, finely minced
4 ounces lump crabmeat, chopped raw shrimp or seafood surimi
3 cups peanut oil or vegetable oil for deep-frying

Heat fish stock, salt, soy sauce, sugar and mirin in a medium-size saucepan over low heat; keep warm. Prepare Crab Fritters. Divide noodles among 4 large noodle bowls. Add spinach leaves and 1 cup hot broth to each bowl. Top with fritters and green onions. Serve at once. Makes 4 servings.

Crab Fritters
In a medium-size bowl, combine flour, cornstarch and baking powder. Whisk in egg white, water, green onions and crab. In a wok or shallow heavy saucepan, heat oil to 365°F (185°C). Slide spoonfuls of batter into hot oil. Fry on both sides until crisp and golden. Drain well. Makes about 10 fritters.

Korean Rice Bowl with Spicy Beef

In Confucian tradition, the Korean homemaker believes the happiness of her family is assured if the father stays well fed. This means three hearty meals a day, each with a bowlful of rice, the common denominator of the meals. To extend the meal, she might stir three tablespoons millet seeds, soaked barley or one cup cooked red or black beans into the simmering rice.

1/2 pound beef sirloin, sliced into thin strips
1 tablespoon soy sauce
1 tablespoon dry white wine
1 teaspoon sesame seed oil
2 garlic cloves, finely minced
1 teaspoon sugar
Pepper to taste
1 cup medium-grain rice, rinsed as directed on page 12
1-1/3 cups water
About 2 tablespoons vegetable oil, more if needed
2 green onions, finely minced
1 tablespoon finely minced fresh gingerroot
1 cup fresh bean sprouts
1/2 teaspoon salt, or to taste
2 tablespoons toasted sesame seeds (page 20)
Kim chee (Korean pickled vegetables)

Marinate meat with soy sauce, wine, sesame seed oil, garlic, sugar and pepper 1 hour. Soak rice with water in a medium-size saucepan 30 minutes. Heat 1 tablespoon of the oil in a medium-size skillet; add green onions and gingerroot and stir-fry 15 seconds. Stir in bean sprouts and salt. Add mixture to rice. Bring to a boil. Cover pan tightly; reduce heat to low. Simmer 15 minutes. Remove from heat; let stand, undisturbed, 10 minutes. Heat a wok or large skillet with remaining oil over medium-high heat. Stir-fry meat 1 to 2 minutes. Spoon rice into 3 large bowls; top each portion with 1/3 of the beef. Garnish with sesame seeds and a small mound of kim chee. Makes 3 servings.

CHILI-STUFFED BLUE CORNMEAL CREPES

I prefer to stuff these crepes with homemade chili, but top-quality ready-made chili will allow you to put this dish together in a hurry. I sometimes arrange the stuffed crepes in individual ovenproof serving dishes to go from the oven directly to the table. I like to spoon spicy green cactus salsa on top of the heated crepes. Serve a green salad or fresh fruit salad on the side.

1 recipe Blue Cornmeal Crepes (page 83)
3 cups chili con carne or chili with beans
2 cups shredded Monterey Jack cheese
1/3 cup thinly sliced green onions
1-1/2 to 2 cups green or red salsa
About 1 cup dairy sour cream
1/4 cup sliced pitted ripe olives
1/4 cup fresh cilantro leaves

Prepare Blue Cornmeal Crepes. Heat oven to 350°F (175°C). Crepes can be arranged on individual dishes or in an oiled 13" x 9" baking dish. Heat chili in a medium-size saucepan over low heat. Spoon about 1/3 cup chili onto each crepe; roll up. Place 2 filled crepes, seam- side down, on each serving dish. Scatter cheese and green onions over each serving. Heat 10 minutes or until the cheese melts. Remove from oven. Spoon salsa and sour cream on top of each serving. Garnish with olives and cilantro. Makes 4 or 5 servings.

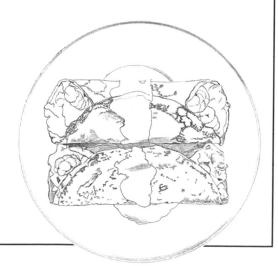

Spice-Scented Couscous with Saffron Chicken

"Couscous" refers to steamed grains of semolina as well as to the complete dish which includes cooked meats, vegetables, a rich broth and a spicy red pepper seasoning paste called harissa. While this recipe does not present the authentic technique of orchestrating a traditional couscous feast, it captures the spirit of the dish through the elusive, exotic flavors.

2 tablespoons butter or margarine
1 medium-size onion, sliced
2 garlic cloves, minced
1 (2-1/2- to 3-lb.) chicken, rinsed, patted dry
4 cups water
2 pinches of saffron threads
3 or 4 parsley sprigs
3 carrots, cut into 1/2-inch pieces
2 zucchini, cut into 1/2-inch pieces
1 recipe Spice-Scented Couscous (page 75)
3 tablespoons raisins, plumped in sherry or hot water
1/4 cup toasted slivered almonds
Mint or cilantro sprigs
Harissa or sambal oelek (hot chile sauce)

Heat butter in a heavy pot over medium heat. Add onion and garlic; sauté 1 minute. Add chicken, water, saffron and parsley. Simmer, covered, 30 minutes. Add carrots; cook 15 minutes. Add zucchini; cook 10 minutes. Keep vegetables and chicken warm. Prepare Spice-Scented Couscous; stir in raisins and almonds. Spoon onto a large serving platter. Place chicken and vegetables on top. Garnish with mint or cilantro. Strain warm broth; serve in a bowl to spoon over couscous. Serve with harissa. Makes 4 servings.

CREOLE SHRIMP SAUCE

This sauce begins with a roux, a browned flour and fat mixture which lends a distinctive taste to Cajun dishes. No Cajun cook would be caught without a generous supply in the kitchen. The sauce is even better made a day ahead; add the shrimp when you reheat the sauce. Besides rice, spoon the sauce over squares of hot polenta, millet pilaf or ricelike grains of cooked kamut.

1/4 cup vegetable oil
1/4 cup all-purpose flour
1 medium-size onion, finely chopped
1 small green bell pepper, finely chopped
1 celery stalk, finely chopped
2 garlic cloves, minced
1 (28-oz.) can plum tomatoes drained, chopped
2 cups Homemade Chicken Stock (page 24), canned broth or shrimp stock
1/2 cup tomato paste
1 teaspoon salt
1/4 teaspoon black pepper
1 bay leaf
1 tablespoon chopped fresh thyme leaves or 1 teaspoon dried leaf thyme
2 teaspoons sugar
4 tablespoons minced fresh parsley
1 recipe Cooked Long-Grain Rice (page 14)
1-1/4 pounds medium-size shrimp, peeled, cleaned

Heat oil in a heavy saucepan; add flour. Cook over the lowest heat, stirring constantly, 15 to 20 minutes or until the roux is sand-colored and has a nutty smell. Add onion, bell pepper, celery and garlic; stir 5 minutes or until golden and vegetables are soft. Add tomatoes, stock, tomato paste, salt, black pepper, bay leaf, thyme, sugar and 2 table-spoons of the parsley into rice. Cover and simmer 45 minutes, stirring often. Prepare rice; stir remaining parsley. Keep warm. Add shrimp to sauce; simmer 5 minutes or until shrimp are cooked. Serve over rice. Makes 2 or 3 servings.

TURKISH GRAPE LEAVES STUFFED WITH LAMB, BULGUR & MINT

To remove excess salt from the grape leaves, blanch them in boiling water one minute. Arrange each serving of grape leaves on a bed of rice pilaf flavored with lemon peel and fresh dill. Pass a plate of lemon wedges and a bowl of fresh plain yogurt to spoon on top.

2 cups Homemade Chicken Stock (page 24), canned broth or water
1/3 cup bulgur wheat
1 pound ground lamb or beef
1/4 cup tomato paste
2 tablespoons dry white wine
4 green onions, minced
2 garlic cloves, minced
2 tablespoons chopped fresh dill or 2 teaspoons dried dill
1/4 cup minced fresh mint leaves
2 tablespoons minced fresh parsley
1 teaspoon salt
1/2 teaspoon pepper
About 40 preserved grape leaves, separated, rinsed, blanched
Juice of 1 lemon

In a small saucepan, bring 1 cup of the stock to a boil. In a medium-size bowl, soak bulgur in boiling stock 45 minutes. In a large bowl, combine lamb with bulgur and all the remaining ingredients, except grape leaves and lemon juice. Lay out a grape leaf, vein-side up, with the stem closest to you. Place about 1 tablespoon filling at the base of the leaf. Roll up, tucking in the sides to form a small package. Fill remaining leaves. Pack stuffed leaves tightly in 2 medium-size skillets. Add 1/2 cup stock to each skillet; sprinkle with lemon juice. Place large plates on top to weigh down the stuffed leaves. Simmer over low heat about 1 hour or until leaves are tender. Add stock or water as needed. Serve warm or at room temperature. Makes 4 servings.

YAKITORI DONBURI

Japanese donburi is a rice meal in a bowl. This recipe features a delicious topping of yakitori, a popular grilled chicken snack available in restaurants and street stalls throughout Japan. Dee Bradney sends this creative family favorite from her home in Okinawa, Japan.

4 chicken breast halves, skinned, boned, cut into 10 pieces
2 bunches green onions, white parts only, cut into 1-inch pieces
1/4 cup soy sauce
2 tablespoons mirin
1 teaspoon sugar
2 teaspoons grated fresh gingerroot
1 recipe Cooked Medium-Grain Rice (page 17)
1/2 cup frozen green peas
1/2 teaspoon sesame seed oil
4 teaspoons toasted sesame seeds (page 20)

Soak 13 (8- to 10-inch) bamboo skewers in water. Thread 3 chicken cubes alternately with 2 pieces green onion on each skewer. Place in a shallow pan; add soy sauce, mirin, sugar and gingerroot. Marinate 30 minutes. Prepare rice. After rice cooks 15 minutes, sprinkle peas on top. Cover; let stand 10 minutes. Preheat a charcoal grill. Remove chicken skewers from pan; reserve marinade. Grill 3 to 5 minutes or until chicken is cooked through, using marinade as a baste. Turn 1 or 2 times. Toss peas with rice; spoon into large bowls. On top of each portion, push the grilled chicken and onions from 3 skewers. Sprinkle with sesame seeds. Makes 4 servings.

Vegetarian Entrees

Grains are the basis of the vegetarian diet. In a meatless diet, grains are an important source of protein, B-complex vitamins and minerals. They are complex carbohydrates and are an excellent source of natural fiber. All this, plus they are low in fat!

But unlike most animal proteins, grain proteins are incomplete, and do not contain amounts of all nine essential amino acids; the building blocks of protein. However, if grains are combined with protein-rich legumes, nuts or seeds, the foods complement each other nutritionally and supplement each other's protein deficiencies.

Cuban Rice with Black Beans (page 58) is not only a good source of "complementary proteins," but offers a range of complementary flavors and textures. Include a cup of milk or a milk product with your meal to maximize the amount of protein and help meet your daily requirement for vitamin B_{12}, an essential vitamin unavailable from plant sources.

Some of the most delicious vegetarian dishes spring from Asia and the Middle East. In these grain-based societies, bland grains are well-seasoned with spices and aromatic vegetables. Emerald Fried Rice (page 65) contains tofu, a soybean food which is a complete protein.

These dishes are good for the vegan diet (no meat, dairy products or eggs) or the ovo-lacto vegetarian diet (no meat, but dairy products and eggs are allowed). They are especially useful for part-time vegetarians who want to reduce the amount of meat in their diet along with fats and calories. With these tasty dishes, a meatless meal or two each week might become a way of life. Whichever diet is your lifetime commitment, keep it nutritionally balanced. Daily portions of grains, legumes, dairy products, fruits and vegetables are all necessary for continuing good health.

Pear & Gorgonzola Quesadillas

The quesadilla, a wheat-flour tortilla and cheese snack, makes a splendid sandwich for supper or lunch. In this version, a pair of flour tortillas is stuffed with cheese, sliced pears, sage and walnuts, then sautéed in butter until the cheese is melted.

10 (8-inch) fresh flour tortillas
3 cups shredded Monterey Jack cheese (12 oz.)
4 ounces Gorgonzola or Blue Castello cheese, finely crumbled
1 firm pear, peeled, cored, thinly sliced
25 fresh sage leaves
1/3 cup finely chopped walnuts
1/4 cup butter or margarine

Place 5 tortillas on a flat surface. Sprinkle each with Monterey Jack cheese and blue cheese. Arrange pear slices and sage leaves on top; sprinkle with walnuts. Top with 5 tortillas; press gently. Brush with butter. Heat an electric griddle or a nonstick skillet over medium-high heat. Brush an area about the size of a tortilla with butter. With a large spatula, lift a quesadilla to the hot griddle. Press with a spatula while cooking or weight down with a heavy plate. When golden-brown, brush the top with butter; turn and cook until golden-brown and the cheeses melt. Cut each quesadilla into 4 wedges. Makes 5 servings.

Rice & Chickpea Pullao

A Pakistani friend shared this recipe with me when our husbands attended the Navy War College in Newport, Rhode Island. Cook the onions slowly until they turn light-brown and slightly caramelized. This is essential to the color and flavor of the finished dish. On the side, I serve fried eggplant slices topped with raita, plain yogurt mixed with chopped cucumber, minced garlic and ground cumin.

2 cups imported basmati or American-style basmati white rice, rinsed (page 12)
1-1/2 cups water
1/4 cup Ghee (page 21), butter or vegetable oil
1 large onion, cut into quarters, sliced paper-thin
1 (1-inch) piece cassia bark or cinnamon stick
3 whole peppercorns
3 whole cardamom pods
2 whole cloves
2 cups cooked chickpeas (3/4 cup dried) or 1 (16-oz.) can chickpeas, rinsed
2 cups Homemade Chicken Stock (page 24), canned chicken broth or water
1 teaspoon salt, or to taste

Place rice and water in a medium-size bowl; soak 30 minutes or until chalky. In a medium-size saucepan, heat Ghee over medium-low heat. Add onion; cook 15 minutes. Add spices. Cook onions 5 more minutes or until they become golden-brown. Drain rice well; reserve liquid. Stir rice into onion mixture; cook 1 minute. Stir in reserved liquid, chickpeas, chicken stock and salt. Bring to a boil. Cover pan tightly. Reduce heat to low. Cook 15 minutes or until the rice is tender and dry. Remove pan from heat. Let rice stand, undisturbed, 10 minutes. Fluff rice. Makes 6 servings.

Cuban Rice with Black Beans

The classic dish "Moros y Cristianos" is a mixed rice and black bean dish which reminds Cubans of their strong Spanish heritage. Here, the richly flavored black beans are ladled on top of the golden rice.

6 cups Homemade Chicken Stock (page 24), or canned broth
2 cups dried black beans, rinsed, soaked overnight, drained
1 large onion, chopped
1 green bell pepper, chopped
2 large garlic cloves, minced
About 1/4 cup extra-virgin olive oil
2 teaspoons ground cumin
1 tablespoon chopped fresh oregano or 1 teaspoon dried leaf oregano
Salt and black pepper to taste
Red-wine vinegar to taste
1/4 cup minced fresh cilantro leaves
1 recipe Saffron Rice (page 68)

Combine stock, beans, onion, bell pepper, garlic, the oil, cumin and oregano in a large pot. Bring to a boil. Cover pan, reduce heat and simmer 2 hours or until beans are tender. Puree 1 cup beans and liquid in a food processor; stir back into the pot. Season with salt, black pepper, vinegar and cilantro. Prepare Saffron Rice. Spoon rice onto each plate; ladle beans on top. Drizzle each serving with additional vinegar and olive oil. Makes 3 or 4 servings.

Spicy Lentil Puree
with Fragrant Basmati Pilaf

In India, protein-rich lentils form the basis of the vegetarian diet. Cooked into a puree, or dahl, lentils become a nutritious, satisfying meal when paired with rice. Onions, chiles, garlic and spices add flavor to the bland yet pleasant-tasting dahl. For a smoother puree, process the lentils briefly in a blender or food processor.

2 cups red lentils (masoor dahl), picked over, rinsed in cool water, drained
6 cups water
1/3 cup vegetable oil
1 tablespoon black mustard seeds or 1-1/2 teaspoons cumin seeds
2 medium-size onions, chopped
4 large garlic cloves, minced
1 teaspoon finely minced fresh gingerroot
1/2 teaspoon ground turmeric
1 small fresh red chile (optional), seeded, minced
1 large tomato, seeded, finely chopped
1 teaspoon salt, or to taste
3 tablespoons chopped fresh cilantro leaves
1 recipe Fragrant Basmati Pilaf (page 18)

In a large bowl, soak lentils in water 30 minutes; drain well. In a large pot, simmer lentils and the 6 cups water over medium heat. Partially cover pot. Cook, stirring often, 35 to 40 minutes or until lentils lose their shape. In a wok or medium-size skillet, heat oil over medium-high heat. Add mustard seeds; stir until they pop. They may splatter; cover with a lid or a mesh splatter-cover. Reduce heat. Add onions, garlic, gingerroot, turmeric and chile, if using. Stir 4 minutes. Stir into lentil puree. Stir in tomato, salt and cilantro. Serve over rice. Makes 6 to 8 servings.

CRISPY FRIED POTATO, BULGUR & WALNUT BALLS

This Middle Eastern vegetarian treat is made with herb-flavored mashed potatoes, bulgur and walnuts which are shaped into balls and deep-fried. If you wish, shape the mixture into six (3-inch) patties, dust with flour, then sauté in a little olive oil and butter until crisp. On the side, serve an eggplant or zucchini dish and a mixed green salad with an olive oil dressing.

2-1/2 cups unseasoned mashed cooked potatoes (2 large potatoes)
1/2 recipe Soaked Bulgur (page 18)
1/4 cup all-purpose flour
3 green onions, minced
2 garlic cloves, minced
1/4 cup each minced fresh cilantro and minced fresh parsley
1/3 cup finely chopped walnuts or pecans
1-1/2 teaspoons salt
1/2 teaspoon ground allspice, cinnamon or cumin
4 cups vegetable oil for deep-frying
All-purpose flour for dusting

In a large bowl, combine all ingredients except oil and flour for dusting. In a wok or shallow heavy saucepan, heat oil to 360°F (180°C). Measure mixture into 6 generous 1/2-cup portions; shape each portion into 3 balls. Dust potato balls with flour. Deep-fry 4 or 5 at a time 4 minutes or until crisp and medium-brown. Turn several times for even browning. Drain well. Serve warm. Makes 18 balls or 6 servings.

SMOKY MOUNTAIN CORN BREAD CASSEROLE

Upper East Tennesseans make corn bread with stone-ground white cornmeal and no sugar. For a crisp, golden crust, bake the corn bread in a well-seasoned cast-iron skillet, preferably one you inherited from your grandmother! Here, the corn bread is baked over pinto beans to re-create an old Tennessee favorite. The tomato-chile blend lends a contemporary taste. Serve with chopped, sweet onion, chow chow (cabbage relish) or a dash of hot pepper sauce.

1 tablespoon vegetable oil
1 small onion, minced
3 cups cooked pinto beans with liquid or 2 (15-oz.) cans pinto beans, undrained
Salt and pepper to taste
1 (10-oz.) can diced tomatoes and green chiles or chunky salsa
1/2 cup all-purpose flour
1 cup white cornmeal, preferably stone ground
1-1/2 teaspoons baking powder
1/2 teaspoon baking soda
1/2 teaspoon salt
1 large egg
1 cup buttermilk
3 tablespoons melted butter or vegetable oil

Heat oil in a large skillet over medium-low heat. Add onion; sauté 4 minutes. Stir in beans, salt, pepper and tomatoes and chiles. Include at least 1/2 cup bean liquid. Keep mixture hot. In a large bowl, sift flour, cornmeal, baking powder, baking soda and the 1/2 teaspoon salt. In a small bowl, whisk together egg, buttermilk and butter. Stir into flour mixture, just until dry ingredients are moistened. Pour beans into a medium-size cast-iron skillet or a 9-inch baking pan; top with the batter. Bake 25 minutes or until corn bread is done. Makes 4 servings.

ARABIC PIZZAS

Flat, soft, round Arabic breads are brushed with aromatic Thyme Oil before the toppings are added. A tender blanched grape leaf or a few thin slices of fried eggplant are a delicious addition before the cheese. Serve the pizzas with a large Greek salad for a light, yet satisfying meal.

Thyme Oil, see below
1 recipe Whole-Wheat Pocket Breads (page 82)
2 to 3 ounces crumbled feta cheese
2 cups shredded mozzarella cheese (8 oz.)
1 to 2 ounces sun-dried tomato halves, rehydrated, cut into strips
1/2 cup pitted, sliced oil-cured olives
1/2 cup toasted pine nuts or 1/3 cup toasted sesame seeds (page 20)

Thyme Oil:
1/4 cup olive oil
2 tablespoons finely minced red onion
1 tablespoon crumbled, dried leaf thyme
2 garlic cloves, finely minced
Salt and pepper to taste

Prepare Thyme Oil; set aside. Prepare Whole-Wheat Pocket Breads. Place dough circles on greased baking sheets. Allow the bread to rise only 15 minutes. Preheat oven to 350°F (175°C). Brush the top of each bread with a generous amount of Thyme Oil. Sprinkle equal portions of feta cheese, mozzarella cheese, tomatoes, olives and pine nuts over each dough circle. Bake 8 to 10 minutes, until the bottom of the pizzas are golden-brown and cheeses are bubbly. Makes 6 servings.

Thyme Oil
In a small bowl, combine all ingredients 2 hours in advance. Makes 1/3 cup.

Spicy Mediterranean Vegetable Stew

Spoon portions of this garden-fresh curried vegetable stew over Spice-Scented Couscous (page 75) or Fragrant Basmati Pilaf (page 18). Serve a dab of harissa, sambal oelek or any other fiery chile sauce on the side. Clean, cut and assemble the vegetables before you begin to cook.

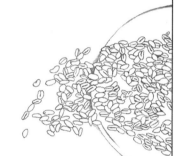

2 tablespoons Ghee (page 21) or butter
1 medium-size onion, chopped
1 small green bell pepper, chopped
1 teaspoon minced fresh gingerroot
2 garlic cloves, minced
1/2 teaspoon each whole cumin seeds and ground cardamom
1/4 teaspoon ground turmeric
3 (4-oz.) purple Oriental eggplants, cut into chunks
3 new potatoes, scrubbed, cut into eighths
10 to 12 baby carrots, parboiled 3 minutes
4 or 5 plum tomatoes, cut into chunks
2 (16-oz.) cans chickpeas, drained, rinsed
1 cup Chicken Stock with Ginger (page 24) or canned broth
2 tablespoons each minced fresh parsley and cilantro
Salt and black pepper to taste
1/3 cup coarsely chopped cashews, peanuts or toasted pine nuts
2 tablespoons extra-virgin olive oil
Harissa, sambel oelek or other hot chile sauce to taste

Heat the Ghee in a large saucepan over medium heat. Add onion, bell pepper, gingerroot, garlic and spices; sauté 3 minutes. Stir in eggplants, potatoes, carrots, tomatoes and chickpeas. Add stock. Cover pan; cook 30 minutes or until vegetables are tender and stew is thick. Stir in herbs, salt and pepper. Top each portion with cashews and a drizzle of olive oil. Serve hot chile sauce on the side. Makes 4 servings.

ZUCCHINI STUFFED WITH BROWN RICE, PINE NUTS & FRESH HERBS

This delicious, low-calorie dish is a summertime treat. I garnish the serving plates with red and yellow nasturtiums from my garden. On the side, I serve thin slices of marinated hothouse cucumbers on a bed of peppery nasturtium leaves. If I have a summer squash in bloom, I like to include yellow squash blossoms stuffed with low-fat cottage cheese mixed with fresh chives. This dish is nice when made with Riz Cous, brown rice grains which resemble couscous.

6 medium-size zucchini, cut in half lengthwise, steamed until crisp-tender
2 tablespoons olive oil
1 small onion, finely chopped
1 cup Basic Brown Rice (page 13), preferably made with light-bran rice
2-1/4 cups Homemade Chicken Stock (page 24)
1 tablespoon fresh lemon juice
1/4 pound fresh mushrooms, diced into small pieces
1/2 cup diced red bell pepper
1 tablespoon finely chopped fresh mint leaves
2 tablespoons minced parsley
1/3 cup toasted pine nuts
Salt and black pepper to taste
1/2 cup freshly grated Parmesan cheese

With a spoon, scoop out and discard seeds and some pulp from zucchini. Set shells aside. In a medium-size saucepan heat 1 tablespoon of the oil over medium heat. Add onion; sauté 3 minutes. Add rice; cook, stirring, 1 minute longer. Add chicken stock and lemon juice. Bring mixture to a boil. Cover pan; reduce heat to low. Cook 15 minutes. Remove from heat. Allow pan to stand, undisturbed, 10 minutes. Heat a medium-size skillet over medium-high heat. Add remaining oil. Add mushrooms and bell pepper; sauté until tender and blend into rice. Stir in mint, parsley, pine nuts, salt and black pepper. Preheat oven to 375°F (190°C). Place zucchini into a large, oiled baking dish. Spoon rice mixture into shells; sprinkle each with 2 teaspoons cheese. Bake 10 minutes or until hot. Makes 4 servings.

EMERALD FRIED RICE

This is a version of a dish I enjoyed in Taipei. Refrigerate the cooked rice on a baking sheet two to three hours or up to one day in advance of the cooking time. Don't use converted rice; the grains become too hard. Be sure your wok is well-seasoned to minimize rice and the egg from sticking to it. For a Thai taste, stir one teaspoon spicy-hot Thai green curry paste in with the onion and garlic.

4 tablespoons vegetable oil
8 ounces firm tofu, cut into 1/2-inch cubes, drained on paper towels
2 green onions, minced
2 garlic cloves, minced
2 cups finely shredded, tender, outer green cabbage leaves
1 recipe Oriental-Style Long Grain Rice (page 14), cooked and chilled
1/3 cup frozen green peas, thawed
1 tablespoon thin soy sauce
2 large eggs, slightly beaten
1 tablespoon minced fresh cilantro
Salt to taste

In a wok or large skillet, heat 2 tablespoons of the oil over medium heat. Add tofu; fry, turning gently, until lightly browned. Remove from pan; drain well. Wipe wok clean; reheat and add remaining oil. Add onions and garlic; stir-fry 30 seconds. Add cabbage; stir-fry 2 minutes. Reduce heat slightly. Mix in rice, peas and soy sauce. Make a well in the center and add eggs; cook until soft scrambled. Toss lightly to mix ingredients. Stir in tofu and cilantro. Add salt to taste. Makes 2 or 3 servings.

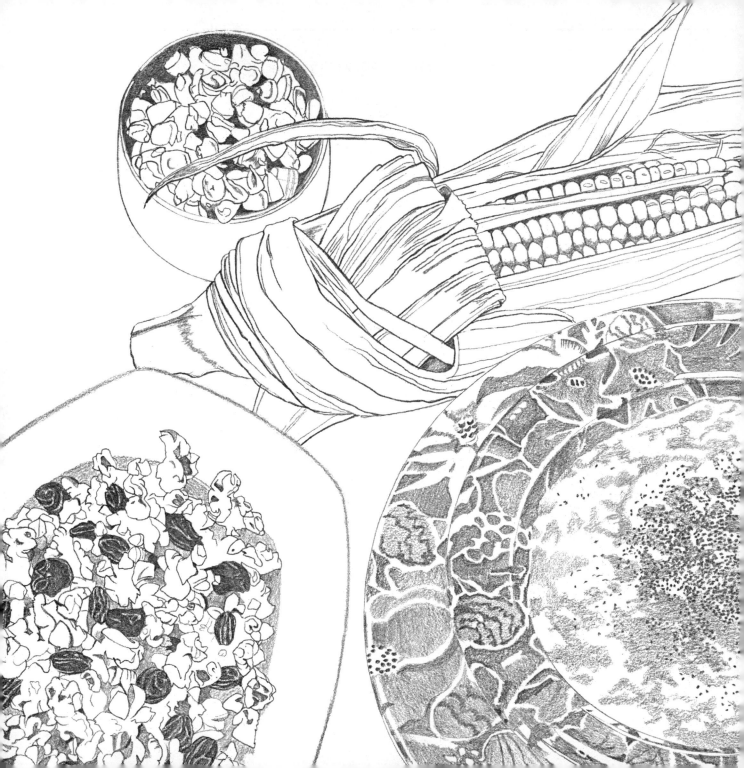

Side Dishes

Corn is an old English word once used to refer to the staple grain of a country. Wheat would have been the "corn" of a culture which primarily ate wheat. In the New World, Indians called today's corn plant "maize," while explorers called it "Indian corn." Worshipped as "Our Mother" by many Native American tribes, maize was important in the North, Central and South America. It became equally important to the white men coming to this new land, eventually sparking the growth of American technology. Country Corn Pudding (page 70) is a satisfying side dish made with sweet corn. Freshly picked or fresh/frozen corn tastes best. Corn begins losing sweetness, turning starchy the moment it is removed from the stalk.

Native Americans discovered that ash (lime) could be added to dried corn to soften the kernels, making grinding and digestion easier. The treated kernels, called hominy, are especially delicious in Southern-Style Creamed Hominy (page 69). One nutritional note on hominy: lime releases the niacin in corn, making it available to the body for absorption.

Grits, coarsely ground dried corn, were originally ground from hominy. It is the quintessential Southern dish, cooked like porridge and served as a side dish with breakfast eggs in the south. Y'all Come Carolina Grits Soufflé (page 76) is an epicurean version which makes a fine side dish for game birds, poultry or ham.

Corn made its way to Europe and in the mid-seventeenth century became popular in Italy. Northern Italians have a penchant for polenta, a golden cornmeal mush which is traditionally poured onto a wooden board to cool. Portions are served plain or with a tomato-based sauce. To savor the flavor of Italy, prepare the recipe Polenta with Spinach, Mushrooms & Fontina (page 79).

Almost any whole grain can be made into pilaf. In fact, it is only slightly more trouble than cooking the plain boiled grain, and far more delicious. Before grain and liquid are combined in the pot, the grain is cooked in oil or butter two minutes or until it turns golden-brown. The pilaf will have a nutty flavor and light, separate grains. Stock or water with a little white wine makes a superbly flavored pilaf.

SAFFRON RICE

Serve this golden Spanish-style pilaf instead of plain white rice for a special meal. Create your own variation by adding one or two of the following ingredients: toasted almonds, golden raisins, chopped tomato, spicy sausage, green peas, pimentos, capers, cilantro, artichoke hearts or sliced green olives.

1/2 teaspoon saffron threads
1/4 cup boiling water
2 tablespoons olive oil
1 medium-size onion, minced
1/2 red bell pepper, diced into small pieces
2 garlic cloves, minced
1 cup long-grain rice
1-3/4 cups Homemade Chicken Stock (page 24), canned broth or water
2 tablespoons minced fresh parsley
Salt and black pepper to taste

Crumble saffron into a small bowl; add boiling water. In a medium-size saucepan over medium-low heat, heat oil. Add onion, bell pepper and garlic; sauté 3 minutes. Add rice; stir 1 minute. Add stock and saffron with water. Cover pan; simmer 15 minutes. Remove from heat and let stand, undisturbed, 10 minutes. Stir in parsley, salt and pepper. Makes 4 servings.

SOUTHERN-STYLE CREAMED HOMINY

Hominy is dried corn treated with a lye solution to create a special taste and texture. Simmered in cream and butter, canned hominy becomes meltingly tender and tastes divine. Prepared this way, hominy often shows up on the finest southern sideboards.

2 (15-oz.) cans white or yellow hominy, drained
2/3 cup whipping cream
1/4 cup unsalted butter
1/2 teaspoon salt
1/4 cup grated Parmesan cheese
1 tablespoon snipped fresh chives
Hot pepper sauce to taste

In the top pan of a double boiler, combine hominy, cream, butter and salt. Place over a double boiler base filled with simmering water. Cook 30 minutes or until cream is absorbed. Stir in cheese, chives and pepper sauce. Makes 5 or 6 servings.

Variation

Southwestern-Style Creamed Hominy: Prepare as directed above, but omit chives and Parmesan cheese. Add 2 diced, peeled, roasted mild green chiles and 1/2 cup shredded longhorn Cheddar cheese or pepper-Jack cheese or 2 ounces diced bel paese cheese. Stir until cheese melts.

COUNTRY CORN PUDDING

East Tennessee-Western Carolina mountain cooks used to cut corn from the cob with a homemade "corn gritter." This handy kitchen tool was made from a piece of tin punched full of nail holes to create a rough grating side. The "gritted meal" was used for pudding and breads. I recommend a small, sharp knife to scrape or cut the kernels off the cob.

4 tablespoons unsalted butter
1/2 cup finely chopped onion
1/4 cup minced green bell pepper
2 tablespoons all-purpose flour
1 cup half and half or milk
2 large eggs, separated
2 cups freshly cut whole-kernel corn (3 ears) or 2 cups frozen
    whole-kernel corn, thawed
1 teaspoon salt
1 tablespoon sugar

Preheat oven to 350°F (175°C). Spread 1 tablespoon butter inside a 2-quart casserole dish; set aside. Melt remaining butter in a medium-size saucepan over medium-low heat. Add onion and bell pepper; sauté 4 minutes. Stir in flour; cook 1 minute. Gradually whisk in milk. Cook 3 or 4 minutes or until thick. Remove from heat, whisk in egg yolks, 1 at a time. Stir in corn and salt. Scrape corn mixture into a large bowl. Cool slightly. In a medium-size bowl, beat egg whites with sugar until stiff but not dry. Fold into corn mixture. Pour into prepared pan. Bake 30 minutes or until puffy and golden-brown. Makes 4 or 5 servings.

WILD PECAN RICE SEASONED WITH SAUSAGE, FENNEL SEEDS & FRESH SAGE

Louisiana Wild Pecan® rice doesn't contain pecans but it has a rich nutty flavor and aroma. It has all the nutrients of brown rice, yet cooks in half the time. Serve this flavorful side dish with beef, ham or poultry.

1-1/2 tablespoons unsalted butter or margarine
1 cup Wild Pecan rice or other long-grain rice
2 cups Homemade Chicken Stock (page 24) or canned broth
1/4 pound spicy bulk sausage
1/2 teaspoon fennel seeds
4 green onions, thinly sliced
1/3 cup diced red bell pepper
1 medium-size yellow squash, cut into quarters, sliced 1/4 inch thick
1 small zucchini, cut into quarters, sliced 1/4 inch thick
1 tablespoon minced fresh sage leaves or 1 teaspoon dried leaf sage, crumbled
2 tablespoons minced fresh parsley
1/3 cup toasted chopped pecans
Salt and black pepper to taste

In a heavy saucepan, melt butter over medium heat. Add rice; sauté 30 seconds. Stir in stock; bring to a full boil. Cover with a tight-fitting lid; reduce heat to the lowest setting. Cook 20 minutes. As the rice cooks, sauté sausage with fennel seeds in a heavy medium-size skillet, stirring until crumbly. Add onions, bell pepper, yellow squash and zucchini. Cook 1 minute or until vegetables are crisp-tender. Stir in sage and parsley. Remove from heat. Mix in cooked rice, pecans, salt and pepper. Makes 4 or 5 servings.

BROWN RICE, WHEAT BERRY & ONION PILAF

This grain duo is a wonderful change from plain rice or noodles. I like to use American-style basmati brown rice or lightly-milled brown rice instead of regular brown rice. Whole-wheat berries or rye berries provide a chewy texture and lots of extra nutrition. Don't forget to soak the wheat berries in two cups of water the night before you plan to prepare this dish.

1/2 cup whole-wheat berries or whole-rye berries, soaked overnight, drained
About 2 cups Homemade Chicken Stock (page 24) or canned broth
1 recipe Basic Brown Rice (page 13)
2 tablespoons butter or margarine
1 tablespoon vegetable oil
1 medium-size red onion, chopped
1 red bell pepper, roasted, peeled, finely diced
1/4 cup chopped, toasted pecan pieces
1/4 cup minced fresh parsley
2 teaspoons fresh marjoram leaves or thyme
Salt and black pepper to taste

Place soaked, drained wheat berries and 2 cups stock in a small saucepan over medium-high heat. Simmer 50 to 60 minutes or until wheat berries are tender and stock is reduced. Add additional stock if the wheat berries need further cooking. Prepare rice. In a large skillet, heat butter with oil over medium heat. Add onion and bell pepper; sauté 7 or 8 minutes until very soft. Stir in wheat berries, rice, pecans and herbs. Add salt and black pepper. Makes 4 servings.

BUCKWHEAT & PASTA BOWS

The secret to keeping kasha kernels separate is to cook them with an egg white first. Kasha, a favorite Russian grain, has an intense, Old World flavor, which is an acquired taste for some. This dish is a version of a Jewish favorite, kasha varnishkes. Serve on the side with braised pot roast, fresh garden vegetables and lots of rich gravy to spoon on top.

2 tablespoons unsalted butter
1 tablespoon vegetable oil
1 medium-size onion, chopped
1/2 pound button mushrooms, sliced
1 garlic clove, minced
1 cup kasha (roasted buckwheat groats)
1 egg white
1/2 teaspoon salt
2 cups Homemade Beef Stock (page 24), canned broth or water
Salt and pepper to taste
4 ounces dried farfalle (pasta bow ties), cooked following package directions
1 green onion, minced

Melt butter with oil in a medium-size saucepan. Add onion, mushrooms and garlic; sauté 2 to 3 minutes or until soft. Set aside. Mix kasha, egg white and salt in a medium-size skillet. Place over medium heat; cook, stirring, 2 minutes or until kasha grains are dry. Remove from heat. Slowly stir in stock; pour kasha and liquid into saucepan with mushroom mixture. Cover pan. Place over low heat. Simmer 15 minutes or just until tender. Remove from heat. Allow kasha to stand, undisturbed, 5 minutes. Add salt and pepper. Stir in pasta and green onion. Makes 6 servings.

HARVEST RICE WITH CRANBERRIES, WALNUTS & THYME

Wild rice and aromatic Wehani rice are cooked together in chicken stock and apple cider in this recipe. Use tangy cider pressed from fresh apples; it isn't as sweet as apple juice. The cranberries are sugar-glazed to mellow their tart taste.

1 cup fresh cranberries
2 tablespoons sugar
2-1/2 cups Homemade Chicken Stock (page 24) or canned broth
2 tablespoons butter
1 tablespoon vegetable oil
1 medium-size red onion, chopped
1 cup wild rice, rinsed well in a fine mesh strainer
1/2 cup Wehani rice or other long-grain brown rice
1-1/2 cups apple cider
1/2 cup toasted walnut or pecan pieces
1 tablespoon fresh thyme leaves or 1 teaspoon dried leaf thyme, crumbled
1/4 cup minced fresh parsley
Salt and freshly ground pepper to taste

Place cranberries and sugar in a small nonstick skillet over medium-high heat. Shake pan 3 minutes or until sugar melts and cranberries begin to pop. Remove from heat; stir in 2 tablespoons of the chicken stock; cool completely. In a medium-size saucepan, melt butter with oil over medium-high heat. Add onion; sauté 2 minutes. Stir in rice; cook 2 minutes, stirring constantly. Add remaining stock and cider. Reduce heat to low; cover pan tightly. Simmer 40 minutes or until wild rice grains split and become tender, yet retain a slight chewiness. Remove from heat; let stand, undisturbed, 10 minutes. Stir in walnuts, thyme, parsley and cranberries. Add salt and pepper. Makes 5 or 6 servings.

SPICE-SCENTED COUSCOUS

Moroccan couscous is traditionally steamed two or three times in a special pot called a couscousière. This laborious method produces the lightest, most delicious grain. Supermarkets carry boxes of couscous which require less preparation time. The short oven-drying period helps dry and fluff the grain. For flavor and added texture, stir one cup cooked cracked wheat into the couscous. Serve with meats, poultry, fish or spicy stews.

2 tablespoons unsalted butter
1 small onion, minced
1 garlic clove, minced
1/8 teaspoon cumin seeds
Pinch each of ground cinnamon and freshly grated nutmeg
1 cup couscous
2 cups Homemade Chicken Stock (page 24) or canned broth
1 tablespoon minced fresh mint or cilantro
Salt and pepper to taste

Preheat oven to 200°F (95°C). In a large skillet, heat butter over medium-low heat. Add onion, garlic and spices; sauté 4 minutes or until onion is soft. Add couscous; stir 1 minute. Reduce heat to low. Heat stock in a small saucepan; Add 1 cup to couscous; stir gently until absorbed. Add remaining stock; fluff couscous with 2 large spoons 2 to 3 minutes or until remaining stock is absorbed. Spread moist couscous over a large baking sheet. Place in the oven 10 to 12 minutes or until fluffy and dry; stir 1 or 2 times. Stir in mint, salt and pepper. Makes 3 or 4 servings.

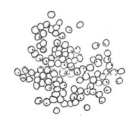

Y'ALL COME CAROLINA GRITS SOUFFLÉ

Charlestonians once referred to grits as "hominy." Grits might be the most controversial food ever to grace a Southerner's table. If you don't believe me, just ask a Northerner! Invite your friends to brunch and treat them to a taste of Southern hospitality along with this creamy hot grits soufflé and country-cured ham or fried quail, fried eggs and hot biscuits.

3 tablespoons butter or margarine
1 small onion, chopped
1 garlic clove, finely minced
1 cup water
1 cup milk
1/2 cup regular grits (not quick-cooking or instant)
3 large eggs, separated
1/4 teaspoon salt, or to taste
Pinch freshly grated nutmeg
2/3 cup shredded sharp Cheddar cheese
2 tablespoons grated Parmesan cheese
3 or 4 drops hot pepper sauce

Butter a 2-quart soufflé dish or casserole dish. Preheat oven to 350°F (175°C). Melt the 3 tablespoons butter in a medium-size saucepan over medium heat. Add onion and garlic; sauté 4 minutes or until tender; set aside. In a medium-size saucepan, bring the water and milk to a boil. Slowly pour in grits, stirring constantly. Reduce heat to low; cook 10 minutes or until thickened. Remove from the heat; slowly whisk in egg yolks, salt, nutmeg, cheeses, hot pepper sauce and onion mixture. Pour grits into a medium-size bowl; cool 5 minutes. Beat egg whites until stiff but not dry. Lighten grits by folding in a small portion of beaten whites. Fold in remaining egg whites. Pour into prepared dish; bake 30 minutes or until puffed and golden. Serve at once. Makes 4 servings.

MILLET, APPLE & CASHEW PILAF IN SQUASH SHELLS

Millet, a tiny golden seed, has an intriguing fragrance and flavor, reminiscent of roasted nuts or an elusive, exotic spice. Served in baked squash shells, this spectacular autumn pilaf goes well with pork, lamb or poultry.

1/4 cup dried currants
2 tablespoons applejack liqueur, rum or apple juice
2 small to medium acorn squash, cut in half, seeds removed
4 tablespoons butter, melted
4 teaspoons brown sugar
1/3 cup thinly sliced green onions
1/2 cup toasted millet
1/4 cup diced red bell pepper
1 tart apple, peeled, cored, diced into small pieces
1/8 teaspoon ground cinnamon, allspice or freshly grated nutmeg
1 cup Homemade Chicken Stock (page 24) or canned broth
1/4 cup finely chopped cashews
Salt and black pepper to taste

Preheat oven to 350°F (175°C). In a small bowl, soak currants in applejack. Slice a thin piece from each squash half so they will stand flat; place in a heavy baking pan. Coat the cut surfaces with 2 tablespoons melted butter; add 1 teaspoon brown sugar to each half. Cover pan with foil. Bake 35 minutes or until the pulp is tender when pierced with a fork. In a medium-size saucepan, heat the remaining butter over medium-high heat. Add onions and sauté 2 minutes. Add millet and cook, stirring, 30 seconds. Stir in bell pepper, apple, cinnamon and currants. Add stock. Cover pan tightly; reduce heat to low. Cook 20 minutes or until liquid is absorbed. Remove from heat. Let stand, undisturbed, 10 minutes. Stir in cashews, salt and black pepper. Spoon pilaf into warm squash shells; serve at once. Makes 4 servings.

OKRA & TOMATO PILAU

Seventeenth century Charleston was the birthplace of the American rice industry. During the American Revolution, the British shipped home the entire rice crop, plus all the seeds. In 1787, Thomas Jefferson smuggled several sacks of Italian rice back to the Carolinas and restocked the rice fields. For a taste of Carolina, try this pilau, a low country dish based on rice.

3 tablespoons olive oil, butter or bacon fat
1 small red onion, minced
1 cup thinly sliced, small, tender okra (about 1/2 lb.)
1 garlic clove, minced
1 cup peeled, chopped tomatoes
1 cup long-grain rice
1-3/4 cups Homemade Chicken Stock (page 24) or canned broth
3 slices crisp-cooked bacon, crumbled
Salt and pepper to taste

Heat oil in a medium-size heavy saucepan over medium heat. Add onion and okra; sauté 5 minutes. Stir in garlic and tomatoes. Cook 1 minute. Stir rice into the mixture, then pour in stock. Bring to a boil. Cover pan and reduce heat to low. Cook 15 minutes. Remove from heat and let stand, undisturbed, 10 minutes. If rice is not quite dry, spread on a baking sheet and dry in a 300°F (150°C) oven about 10 minutes. Add salt and pepper. Serve rice topped with reserved bacon. Makes 4 servings.

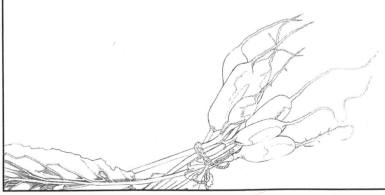

POLENTA WITH SPINACH, MUSHROOMS & FONTINA

Polenta, a staple in Northern Italian kitchens, is served here with a spinach, mushroom and cheese topping. This dish goes well with grilled veal chops, squab or guinea hens.

3 cups water
1/2 teaspoon salt, or to taste
1 cup polenta or coarse-grain yellow cornmeal
2 tablespoons minced prosciutto, fried pancetta, ham or crisp-fried bacon
1/4 cup grated Parmigiano cheese
1/4 teaspoon freshly grated nutmeg
4 tablespoons butter
2 shallots, minced
2 garlic cloves, minced
4 ounces wild mushrooms or button mushrooms, sliced
12 ounces fresh spinach, rinsed, dried, shredded
1 tablespoon all-purpose flour
1-1/4 cups whipping cream or half and half
1 cup shredded Italian fontina cheese

Boil water and salt in a medium-size heavy saucepan. Slowly pour in polenta, whisking constantly. Reduce heat to low. With a wooden spoon, stir 15 minutes or until polenta thickens and pulls away from sides of pan. Stir in prosciutto, Parmigiano cheese, nutmeg and 1 tablespoon of the butter. Pour into a 9- or 10-inch pie pan; set aside. Preheat oven to 350°F (175°C). Wash and dry saucepan; add remaining butter and place over medium heat. Add shallots, garlic and mushrooms; sauté 2 minutes. Stir in spinach. Mix flour with cream; stir into spinach. Simmer until thickened; season to taste. Spread mixture on top of polenta; sprinkle with fontina cheese. Bake 20 minutes until hot and bubbly. Cut into wedges. Makes 6 servings.

Variation

Coat chilled, firm polenta wedges with Parmesan cheese; bake 20 minutes or until golden-brown. Top with the spinach mixture. For an extra-special version, substitute one to two ounces soaked, dried porcini mushrooms for fresh mushrooms.

Breads

Whole grains can be ground into flours for making breads. Breadmaking is an art with special appeal. When we make our own bread, we can produce a healthier, more delicious product and gain a feeling of satisfaction and accomplishment rarely experienced in other areas of cooking. Breadmaking is a tradition we can pass on from generation to generation.

Early breads were made from crushed grains mixed with water. Aristocratic Romans considered white bread a symbol of the politically powerful and added chalk to the flour to insure its whiteness. Today, nutritionally superior whole-wheat flour is the grain of choice. It still contains the bran, germ and endosperm of the wheat kernel. Bran is rich in vitamins, minerals and dietary fiber. The germ is rich in vitamins and minerals. The endosperm, mostly starch, is the critical food supply of a young plant. The recipe Whole-Wheat Pocket Breads (page 82) calls for a portion of whole-wheat flour. This recipe is excellent for beginning bread bakers. Bread dough made entirely of whole-wheat flour is more difficult to work with than one made from a whole-wheat/unbleached flour blend.

Refined white flour, made from pure endosperm, is enriched with many of the vitamins and minerals removed during processing. Unbleached wheat flour is an excellent primary flour for bread baking. It has the most gluten, a protein which gives dough the elasticity to trap carbon dioxide given off by the yeast. This network of gluten is what causes bread to rise properly. Other flours, such as rye flour, whole-wheat flour or buckwheat flour may be protein-rich but contain less gluten. For this reason, white flour should be the foundation of a bread recipe; mix in smaller portions of the other flours. Purchase special flours in natural food stores, specialty markets and food co-ops.

The most delicious and nutritious flours and cornmeals are stone-ground, with the fat-rich germ intact. The grains are not overheated during this milling process, so the nutrients are retained. For the freshest stone-ground flour and cornmeal, order directly from the mills. Refer to the mail order resource list in the back of this book. If the flour or meal is stone-ground, the package will always indicate so. Otherwise, the flour has probably been milled by another process.

WHOLE-WHEAT POCKET BREADS

Pocket bread, or pita bread, puffs magically in the hot oven like a balloon. Slice the breads in half, and stuff each "pocket" with your favorite chicken salad, seafood salad or marinated vegetable salad. The bread rounds can be used as a pizza base or eaten warm with butter and honey. Do not allow the breads to become crisp in the oven; they should stay soft and pliable.

1 (1/4-oz.) package active dry yeast
1 tablespoon sugar
1 cup lukewarm water (110°F, 45°C)
1 tablespoon olive oil
1 teaspoon salt
1-1/2 cups bread flour
1 cup whole-wheat flour

In a large bowl, dissolve yeast and sugar in water. Proof 5 minutes or until foamy. Stir in oil and salt. Beat in flours, 1 cup at a time, until the soft dough pulls away from the sides of the bowl. Knead by machine 2 minutes or knead by hand on a lightly floured surface 5 minutes or until smooth and elastic. Place dough in a large greased bowl; turn to coat surface. Cover lightly; let rise 1 hour or until doubled. Punch down; knead briefly, then shape into 8 smooth balls. Cover; let rest 20 minutes. On a lightly floured surface, roll balls into 7-inch circles. Place on greased, heavy baking sheets. Cover; let rise 10 minutes. Preheat oven to 450°F (230°C). Bake 5 to 7 minutes or just until breads puff and color lightly. Cool completely. Breads may be refrigerated a few days in an airtight plastic bag. Makes 8 pocket breads.

BLUE CORNMEAL CREPES

Blue cornmeal is ground from hand-cultivated blue corn, a Southwestern Indian staple.
Blue corn isn't as easy to work with by hand when making hand-made tortillas,
but it can be transformed into tender crepes with a minimum of fuss. Stuff the crepes with
chili con carne, refried beans, scrambled eggs, creamed turkey or seafood.
The crepes can be prepared ahead and stored in the freezer.

1/2 cup all-purpose flour
1/2 cup blue cornmeal or yellow cornmeal
3/4 cup milk
1/4 cup water
2 large eggs
1 tablespoon butter, melted
1/2 teaspoon ground cumin
1/2 teaspoon salt

In a blender or food processor fitted with the metal blade, combine all ingredients; process until smooth. Pour into a medium-size bowl. Cover; let stand 10 minutes. Heat a crepe pan over medium-low heat. If pan is not nonstick, wipe with vegetable oil. Pour 3 tablespoons batter into pan. Tilt pan to coat bottom. Cook 45 seconds or until crepe is set and lightly browned. Turn and cook 15 seconds more. Remove from pan onto waxed paper. Prepare remaining crepes. Cool completely. Use at once or stack, wrap and refrigerate overnight or freeze for longer storage. Makes 10 crepes.

Maple-Glazed Pecan Cornmeal Muffins

These soft, moist corn muffins are delicious spread with butter and stuffed with thin slices of honey baked ham or smoked turkey. They are equally delicious spread with peach preserves or orange marmalade.

3/4 cup soft-wheat all-purpose flour
1/2 cup white cornmeal
1-1/2 teaspoons baking powder
1/2 teaspoon salt
3 tablespoons sugar
1/4 cup pecan halves, finely chopped
2 large eggs
3/4 cup buttermilk
1/3 cup butter or margarine, melted
Pure maple syrup (optional)

Preheat oven to 375°F (190°C). Lightly oil a 12-cup nonstick muffin pan. Sift flour, cornmeal, baking powder, salt and sugar into a medium-size bowl. Stir in pecans. In a large bowl, whisk eggs and buttermilk. Pour flour mixture over egg mixture. Drizzle butter on top of the two mixtures. With a rubber spatula, blend just until dry ingredients are moistened. Divide batter among 12 muffin cups. Bake 10 to 12 minutes or until done. Run the tops under the broiler for browning, if desired. Brush muffin tops with maple syrup, if using. Serve at once. Leftover muffins reheat well in the microwave. Makes 12 muffins.

POTATO-OATMEAL LOAF WITH SESAME SEEDS & WALNUTS

This moist potato-oatmeal loaf is endowed with an embarrassment of riches: toasted oats, sesame seeds, raisins, walnuts and cinnamon. Enjoy the bread plain or toasted, spread with butter and jam.

1 cup plus 2 tablespoons regular rolled oats, toasted (page 20)
5 tablespoons unsalted butter, room temperature
1/2 cup raisins
1 cup unseasoned mashed cooked potatoes, plus hot potato water from cooking
1/4 cup plus 1 teaspoon honey
1/3 cup toasted sesame seeds (page 20)
1-1/2 teaspoons salt
1 teaspoon ground cinnamon
1/3 cup finely chopped, toasted walnuts (page 20)
2 (1/4-oz.) packages active dry yeast
1/2 cup lukewarm water (110°F, 45°C)
3-1/2 cups all-purpose flour

In a medium-size bowl, place the 1 cup oats, 4 tablespoons of the butter and the raisins; set aside. Prepare mashed potatoes. Measure potato water, adding extra hot water, if necessary, to yield 1 cup. Stir into oat mixture. Stir in potato, 1/4 cup honey, sesame seeds, salt, cinnamon and walnuts. In a large bowl, dissolve yeast in lukewarm water. Proof 5 minutes until foamy. Stir in oat mixture. Beat in flour by the cupful to form a medium-soft dough. Scrape dough onto a floured surface; knead 5 minutes. Place dough in a large greased bowl; turn to coat surface. Cover; let rise 1 hour or until doubled. Punch down; shape into 2 loaves. Grease 2 (8" x 4") loaf pans. Place loaves in greased pans. Make 3 diagonal cuts on top of each loaf. In a small saucepan over low heat, warm remaining butter and 1 teaspoon honey; brush tops of loaves. Sprinkle with remaining oats. Let rise 40 minutes or until double. Preheat oven to 375°F (190°C). Bake 35 minutes or until bread is medium-brown and sounds hollow when tapped on bottom. Cool 10 minutes; remove to a rack to cool. Makes 2 loaves.

SEEDED COTTAGE CHEESE & ONION LOAF

Moist and tender, this fragrant bread is flavored with a trio of dill seeds, caraway seeds and anise seeds. It is baked in a decorative pan to form a handsome bread ring. I created this spectacular loaf for lunch at Ann and Art Buchwald's weekend house party.

2 tablespoons butter or margarine
1 medium-size onion, finely chopped
1 (1/4-oz.) package active dry yeast
1/4 cup lukewarm water (110°F, 45°C)
3/4 cup creamed cottage cheese, room temperature
1 large egg, room temperature
2 tablespoons sugar
1 teaspoon salt
1/4 teaspoon baking soda
1 teaspoon each toasted dill seeds, caraway seeds and anise seeds (page 20)
2-1/2 cups all-purpose flour

Melt butter in a small skillet over medium heat; add onion and sauté 4 minutes or until soft. Set aside. In a large bowl, dissolve yeast in lukewarm water. Proof until foamy. In a small bowl, blend cottage cheese, egg, sugar, salt, soda and toasted seeds. Stir mixture into yeast. Beat in flour by the cupful, to form a soft dough. Beat 2 minutes by machine or knead by hand on a floured surface 5 minutes or until smooth and elastic. Place in a greased bowl; turn to coat surface. Cover; let rise 1 hour or until doubled. Punch down; shape into a 14-inch-long rope. Twist rope; place into an oiled, 6- to 8-cup decorative brioche pan with a tube in the center. Pinch ends to seal. Let dough rise 40 minutes or until almost doubled. Preheat oven to 350°F (175°C). Bake 35 minutes or until golden-brown. Cool 5 minutes. Remove from pan; cool on a wire rack. Makes 1 loaf.

HAM & CHEESE DELI LOAF

This large, impressive loaf tastes like a deli ham and cheese on rye. To create an even more interesting loaf, mix one-third cup cracked whole rye, soaked in ample warm water overnight, into the dough. Spread a fresh slice of this hearty bread with butter or a whole-grain mustard.

3 tablespoons unsalted butter
1 medium-size onion, peeled, chopped
1 tablespoon caraway seeds
1 cup beer, room temperature
1/2 cup milk
2 tablespoons molasses or barley malt syrup
1-1/2 teaspoons salt
1 (1/4-oz.) package active dry yeast
1/4 cup lukewarm water (110°F, 45°C)
3 cups bread flour
1 cup rye flour
1/2 cup finely chopped ham, corned beef or pepperoni
1/2 cup shredded Cheddar or Swiss cheese

Melt butter in a medium-size saucepan over medium-low heat. Add onion and caraway seeds; sauté 5 minutes or until golden-brown. Remove pan from heat; stir in beer, milk, molasses and salt. Cool slightly. In a small bowl, dissolve yeast in lukewarm water. Proof 5 minutes or until foamy. Pour onion mixture into a large bowl. Beat in yeast and flours. Dough will be sticky. Knead 2 minutes in the mixer. Or, scrape dough onto a lightly floured surface; knead 5 to 8 minutes. Place into a greased bowl; turn to coat surface. Cover; let rise 1 hour or until doubled. Punch down; let rise again. Roll into a 10- to 11-inch circle; sprinkle with ham and cheese. Roll up tightly to enclose filling, thin coil to form a round loaf. Pinch tightly to seal edges. Place on a baking sheet with large seams down. Make 3 diagonal slashes on top of dough. Let rise 40 minutes. Preheat oven to 375°F (190°C). Bake 30 minutes or until crusty and medium-brown. Cool completely. For soft crust, brush with melted butter. Makes 1 loaf.

TRITICALE HONEY PECAN TWIST

America's "amber waves of grain" include triticale, a manmade hybrid developed in the 1960s. The high-protein grain is a cross between durum wheat, winter wheat and rye. The flour has a very natural nutty flavor which tastes wonderful baked into breads.

1 (1/4-oz.) package active dry yeast
1/4 cup lukewarm water (110°F, 45°C)
3 tablespoons honey
1 teaspoon salt
2 tablespoons butter or margarine
2 tablespoons wheat germ
3/4 cup milk, scalded
1 cup triticale flour
1/4 cup finely chopped pecans
1-3/4 cups all-purpose flour

In a large mixing bowl, dissolve yeast in lukewarm water. Proof 5 minutes or until foamy. Stir honey, salt, butter and wheat germ into hot milk. Cool until slightly warm. Stir milk mixture, triticale and pecans into yeast. Beat in remaining flour to form a firm dough. Knead 2 minutes by machine or scrape onto a floured surface; knead 5 minutes by hand. When smooth and elastic, place dough into a large greased bowl; turn to coat surface. Cover; let rise 1 hour or until doubled. Punch down. Cut dough in half. Roll each half into a 12-inch-long round rope. Twist the 2 pieces together to form a long twisted rope; pinch ends tightly. Coil twisted rope to form a round loaf; tuck the end securely under the loaf. Place on a greased baking sheet. Let rise 45 minutes. Preheat oven to 350°F (175°C). Bake 35 to 40 minutes or until a wooden pick inserted in center comes out clean. Cool before cutting. Makes 1 loaf.

CREAM & HONEY LOAVES WITH WHEAT BERRIES

Whole-wheat flour, whole-wheat berries and wheat germ are combined to create these nutritious, chewy harvest loaves. The cream adds tenderness and flavor. In place of whole wheat berries. you might use one-half cup cracked wheat berries soaked in one and one-half cups boiling water for one hour. Drain the cracked berries and add them directly to the cream mixture.

1/4 cup wheat berries, soaked in warm water overnight, drained
1 (1/4-oz.) package active dry yeast
1/2 cup lukewarm water (110°F, 45°C)
1/4 cup water
3/4 cup whipping cream
1/3 cup honey
2 teaspoons salt
2 large eggs
2 tablespoons wheat germ
1 cup whole-wheat flour
4 cups unbleached all-purpose flour
1 tablespoon melted butter for brushing on dough

In a small saucepan, simmer the soaked wheat berries in 1 cup water 25 minutes; drain well. In a large bowl, dissolve yeast in lukewarm water. Proof until foamy. In a small saucepan, heat the 1/4 cup water, the cream, honey and salt until lukewarm. Remove from heat; beat in eggs, wheat germ and wheat berries. Pour into yeast mixture. With an electric mixer, beat in flours, 1 cup at a time to make a soft, sticky dough. Beat 2 minutes. Oil hands; scrape dough onto a lightly floured surface. Knead 2 minutes. Place into a large greased bowl; turn to coat surface. Cover; let rise 1 hour or until doubled. Punch down; let rise again. Punch down; on a lightly floured surface, divide dough in half. Shape into 2 loaves. Grease 2 (8" x 4") loaf pans. Place loaves into greased pans. Brush with butter. Let dough rise about 35 minutes. Preheat oven to 350°F (175°C). Bake 30 minutes or until medium golden-brown. Cool before slicing. Makes 2 loaves.

CRÈME DE BANANA MUFFINS
WITH PRALINE LACE

Crème de Banana is a golden liqueur with a heavenly natural banana flavor.
Cake flour gives the muffins a soft, delicate texture.

Praline Lace, see below
1 cup cake flour
1 teaspoon freshly grated nutmeg
1 teaspoon baking powder
1/4 teaspoon baking soda
1/2 teaspoon salt
1/4 cup butter or margarine, room temperature
1/3 cup sugar
1 large egg, room temperature
1/2 cup sour cream or vanilla yogurt, room temperature
1/2 cup mashed ripe banana
3 tablespoons Crème de Banana liqueur

Praline Lace:
1/2 cup sugar
2 tablespoons butter, chilled
2 tablespoons ground pecans
1 teaspoon ground cinnamon

Preheat oven to 375°F (190°C). Line a 12-cup muffin pan with paper liners; coat with vegetable spray. Prepare Praline Lace. In a medium-size bowl, sift together flour, nutmeg, baking powder, soda and salt. Set aside. In a large bowl, cream butter and sugar. Beat in egg and sour cream until smooth. Blend in mashed banana and banana liqueur. Stir in flour mixture just until ingredients are moistened. Spoon into muffin cups. Sprinkle Praline Lace on top of each muffin. Bake 10 to 12 minutes or until muffins are firm and the topping is crunchy. Makes 12 muffins.

Praline Lace
In a small bowl, combine ingredients all until crumbly. Makes about 1/2 cup.

LACY CORNMEAL CAKES

Ash cake, or hoe cake, was a staple food in the early Southern backcountry. One settlement was even named Corncake. Flat cakes of cornmeal and water were wrapped in cabbage leaves and buried under the ashes in the fireplace or placed on a heated hoe. You might want to experiment and stir some minced crisp-fried bacon or minced green onion into this fancy version.

3/4 cup stone-ground cornmeal, preferably white
2 tablespoons all-purpose flour
1/2 teaspoon salt
1 teaspoon sugar
1/2 teaspoon baking soda
1 large egg
1 cup buttermilk
2-1/2 tablespoons vegetable oil, plus extra oil for the griddle

Heat a griddle or large skillet over medium heat. In a large bowl, sift together cornmeal, flour, salt, sugar and soda. In a medium-size bowl, whisk together egg, buttermilk and oil; stir into cornmeal mixture. For each corncake, heat 2 teaspoons oil on the hot griddle; pour on 1/4 cup batter. Cook about 2 minutes or until golden-brown and crispy around the edges. Turn and cook on the other side. Repeat with additional oil and batter. Serve hot with butter. Makes about 8 corncakes.

Breakfast Favorites

Growing up in Tennessee, my mother often reminded me that breakfast was the most important meal of the day. For a Tennessean, a proper breakfast is a splendid repast of country ham, fresh eggs, red-eye gravy, hot biscuits and grits. It is hard to resist this type of bountiful fare, but in the interest of better health, we now reserve meals of such magnitude for leisurely weekend brunches or special occasions. Fiber-rich grain foods and cereals have taken their place, providing an inexpensive, low-fat source of nutrients and energy.

Whole-grain cereals contain high-quality protein, vitamins and minerals. The Scots, long aware of the value of these complex carbohydrates, serve up a hearty bowl of hot oatmeal made from steel-cut oats. Oatmeal retains the nutritional value of whole oats; the outer husks are removed but the germ and bran layers are intact. Rolled oats are made from steamed, softened whole grains which are flattened between steel rollers. Banana-Walnut Oatmeal (page 99) is a luxurious version of the Scotch plain bowl of oats, and one you will make again and again. Scottish steel-cut oats are more coarse; increase the cooking time about 30 minutes. Peaches & Cream Breakfast Pudding (page 98) is a delicious treat made with refined enriched cream of wheat or farina. Boost the cereal's nutritional value by stirring in lysine-rich wheat germ. Other grains can be simmered in water or milk to make a hot breakfast cereal. Try nutty-tasting brown rice or one of the more unusual grains such as buckwheat groats, millet, bulgur, rye or grain sorghum. Wheat germ and sliced fruits will increase the nutritional value; sweetening is subjective and can be added to taste.

Cherry-Almond Granola (page 96) makes a great breakfast ceral or stretch the calories and add a handful to your regular unsweetened hot or cold cereal.

LEMON CREAM MUFFINS WITH RASPBERRIES & ALMOND STREUSEL

Each bite holds a burst of sunny lemon, tangy raspberries and crunchy almond streusel.
For a special treat, use a trio of fresh berries in the muffin batter.

Almond Streusel, see below
2 cups cake flour
1 teaspoon baking powder
1/4 teaspoon salt
1/2 cup butter or margarine, room temperature
3/4 cup sugar
Grated peel of 1 large lemon
1/2 teaspoon almond extract
2 large eggs
1/3 cup sour cream or vanilla yogurt
2/3 cup milk
1 cup fresh raspberries, blackberries or blueberries

Almond Streusel:
1/3 cup sugar
1/4 cup blanched toasted almonds, finely chopped
1/4 cup cake flour
1/4 cup butter or margarine
1/2 teaspoon almond extract

Preheat oven to 350°F (175°C). Line muffin pans with paper baking cups. Prepare Almond Streusel. In a small bowl, sift together flour, baking powder and salt; set aside. In a large bowl, cream butter, sugar, lemon peel and almond extract. Beat in eggs, one at a time. Stir in sour cream. With a spatula, fold in half the flour mixture and 1/3 cup of the milk. Fold in remaining flour mixture, milk and raspberries just until dry ingredients are moistened. Spoon batter into muffin cups. Sprinkle with streusel. Bake 12 to 15 minutes or until done. Makes about 14 muffins.

Almond Streusel
In a medium-size bowl, combine all ingredients until crumbly.

BLACKBERRY BUTTERMILK PANCAKES

Serve these tender, light pancakes with a crock of country butter and a pitcher of warm blackberry syrup. If you prefer, spoon the blackberries on top of each cooked pancake stack instead of cooking them in the batter.

2-1/4 cups soft-wheat flour,
2 tablespoons sugar
2 teaspoons baking powder
1 teaspoon baking soda
1/2 teaspoon salt
1 teaspoon ground cinnamon
1 heaping tablespoon wheat germ
2 large eggs
2 cups buttermilk
1/2 cup sour cream or lowfat yogurt
2 tablespoons melted butter, plus extra for spreading on pancakes
2 cups fresh blackberries or blueberries
Blackberry or blueberry syrup

In a medium-size bowl, combine flour with sugar, baking powder, soda, salt and cinnamon. Sift ingredients together. Stir in wheat germ. In a large bowl, whisk together eggs, buttermilk, sour cream and melted butter; blend into dry ingredients. Heat a griddle or large skillet; wipe lightly with oil. For each pancake, pour 1/3 cup batter onto hot griddle; place 3 or 4 blackberries on top. When bubbles form after 1-1/2 minutes, flip pancake to cook the other side. Remove from griddle when brown and puffed. Serve with butter and syrup. Makes 12 pancakes.

CHERRY-ALMOND GRANOLA

Serve this crunchy granola as a breakfast cereal with yogurt or bake a batch of Cherry-Almond Granola Cookies (page 109). The granola is equally good with any blend of dried fruits and nuts. A portion of rye, barley or wheat flakes can be mixed with the oats.

2 cups regular rolled oats
1 cup coarsely chopped, blanched almonds, chopped walnuts or pecans
1/2 cup shredded coconut
2 tablespoons wheat germ
2 tablespoons Popped Amaranth (page 21)
1 tablespoon toasted millet (page 20)
1 tablespoon sesame seeds
1 teaspoon ground cinnamon
1/4 teaspoon salt
1/2 cup honey, golden syrup, or rice syrup
3 tablespoons safflower oil or canola oil
1 teaspoon pure vanilla extract
3/4 cup dried cherries, cranberries, raspberries, chopped apricots or raisins

In a large bowl, combine oats, almonds, coconut, wheat germ, amaranth, millet, sesame seeds, cinnamon and salt. Preheat oven to 275°F (135°C). Warm honey and oil in a small saucepan; add vanilla. Pour over oat mixture; blend to coat ingredients. Spread onto a nonstick baking sheet. Bake 25 to 30 minutes. Watch carefully; granola should darken only to a warm toasty color. Remove from heat; Mix dried cherries or other fruit into granola. Cool; store in an airtight jar. Makes about 5 cups.

SWEET POTATO BRAN MUFFINS

Breakfast never tasted so good! Start the day with one or two muffins spread with fig preserves or whipped, orange-flavored cream cheese. For an additional energy boost, add a tall glass of fresh-squeezed orange juice. Whole-wheat pastry flour gives these muffins their special soft texture.

1 tablespoon butter or margarine, melted
1/4 cup sugar
1/4 cup finely chopped pecans
1 cup wheat bran cereal
1/2 cup regular rolled oats
1 cup buttermilk
1/2 cup mashed, cooked sweet potato
1/3 cup vegetable oil
1 large egg
1/2 cup light brown sugar
1/4 cup raisins
1/2 cup whole-wheat pastry flour, lightly spooned into measuring cup
2 teaspoons baking powder
1 teaspoon baking soda
1/2 teaspoon salt
1/2 teaspoon each ground cinnamon, nutmeg and allspice

Preheat oven to 350°F (175°C). Stir butter, sugar and pecans in a small bowl until crumbly. Lightly oil a 12-cup nonstick muffin pan. In a large bowl, combine cereal and oats. Stir in buttermilk, sweet potato, oil, egg, brown sugar and raisins. Sift flour, baking powder, soda, salt and spices into a small bowl. Stir into cereal mixture, just until moistened. Spoon batter into muffin cups; sprinkle with pecan mixture. Bake 10 to 12 minutes or until firm and the tops are crunchy. Cool; remove from pan. Makes 12 muffins.

PEACHES & CREAM BREAKFAST PUDDING

This delectable breakfast pudding is made with the enriched wheat cereal, farina.
You might know it under the name, Cream-of-Wheat™. I like to add sliced fresh peaches,
strawberries or a portion of blueberries to each serving.

1-1/2 cups water, plus more if needed
1/2 cup maple syrup, golden syrup or rice syrup
2 tablespoons raisins
1/4 teaspoon ground nutmeg or cinnamon
Pinch salt
2 tablespoons unsalted butter
1/2 cup quick-cooking farina
2 tablespoons toasted wheat germ
3 tablespoons toasted, chopped pecans or walnuts (page 20)
Half and half or milk to taste

In a small saucepan, bring water, syrup, raisins, nutmeg and salt to a boil. In a medium-size saucepan, melt 1 tablespoon of the butter over medium-high heat. Stir in farina and wheat germ; cook 1 to 2 minutes or until lightly toasted. Reduce heat to medium-low. Remove pan from heat. Gradually pour in hot liquid, stirring continually with a long wooden spoon to avoid the hot steam. Cook and stir mixture 3 minutes or until porridge thickens. If too thick, thin with a little water. Pour hot porridge into serving bowls. Top each portion with 1 teaspoon butter, 1 tablespoon pecans and half and half. Makes 3 servings.

BANANA-WALNUT OATMEAL

Plain oatmeal will never taste the same after you try this one. A quick toasting in the oven gives the oats a nutty, intense flavor. Serve the hot oatmeal with a pitcher of milk or a bowl filled with vanilla yogurt for topping.

1-3/4 cups water
Pinch salt
2 tablespoons raisins
1 cup regular rolled oats, toasted (page 20)
1/4 to 1/3 cup maple syrup, rice syrup or brown sugar
2 tablespoons chopped toasted walnuts or pecans
1 tablespoon wheat germ
1/4 teaspoon freshly grated nutmeg
1 small banana, diced
2 or 3 teaspoons unsalted butter

In a medium-size saucepan, bring water, salt and raisins to a boil over medium-high heat. Stir in oats; reduce heat to low. Add remaining ingredients except banana and butter. Stir 4 or 5 minutes or until oats are cooked and porridge is thick. Stir in banana. Divide hot oatmeal among serving bowls. Melt 1 teaspoon butter on top of each serving. Serve at once. Makes 2 or 3 servings.

POTATO SCONES WITH RUM-CREAM GLAZE

As delicious as a pan of warm, glazed cinnamon buns, these spice- and rum-scented scones retain their moist texture even when cold. Freshly mashed potato works best for this bread; do not overwork, as this will develop the starch and cause the potato to become gluey.

3/4 cup mashed cooked potato
3/4 cup buttermilk
2 cups soft-wheat flour
1/2 teaspoon salt
1 tablespoon baking powder
1/2 teaspoon baking soda
1/2 teaspoon each ground cinnamon and freshly grated nutmeg
1 tablespoon sugar
1/3 cup unsalted butter, chilled
1 cup powdered sugar, sifted
1 tablespoon whipping cream
2 to 3 teaspoons dark Myers rum
1/4 cup currants

Preheat oven to 375°F (190°C). In a small bowl, blend potato and buttermilk. Sift flour, salt, baking powder, soda, spices and sugar into a large bowl; cut in butter. Stir in potato mixture until blended. Turn out on a lightly-floured surface; gently knead 10 seconds. Pat dough into a circle, 3/4 inch to 1 inch thick. Cut into 2-1/2-inch rounds. Place into a greased 9- or 10-inch round baking pan. Bake 12 to 15 minutes; tops will brown lightly. Cool 10 minutes. In a small bowl, blend powdered sugar, cream and rum. Frost the scones; sprinkle with currants. Makes 8 scones.

WILD RICE & BUCKWHEAT WAFFLES

The addition of buckwheat flour can increase the nutritive value of foods. Wild rice adds flavor and texture to the waffles; top with creamed turkey, chicken or seafood for a satisfying brunch or supper dish. The waffles are equally delicious served with maple syrup.

1-1/2 cups soft-wheat flour
1 tablespoon baking powder
1/2 teaspoon salt
1 cup milk
1/2 cup sour cream or plain yogurt
2 eggs, separated
6 tablespoons butter, melted
1 tablespoon sugar
1/4 cup buckwheat flour
2 tablespoons finely chopped pecans
1 cup cooked wild rice

Preheat waffle iron; brush lightly with oil. In a large bowl, sift together wheat flour, baking powder and salt. In a medium-size bowl, whisk milk, sour cream, egg yolks and butter. Beat egg whites with sugar until stiff but not dry. Stir milk mixture into dry ingredients. Gently stir in buckwheat flour, pecans and wild rice. Fold in egg whites. For each waffle, pour 3/4 cup batter onto hot waffle iron; cook until crisp and brown. To keep waffles crisp, place them on a rack in an oven preheated to 200°F (95°C). Makes 5 waffles.

Desserts

Cookies are a holiday remembrance where one size really does fit all! Baking cookies is an annual holiday ritual observed in homes throughout the world. Surprise someone special in your life with a basket of crunchy Cherry-Almond Granola Cookies (page 109) or a tin of Harlequin Shortbread (page 104).

Baked goods are a great way to introduce a new, unfamiliar grain to your family. Crunchy Popped Amaranth (page 23) replaces nuts in Aztec Cookies with Amaranth (page 111). Amaranth expands and resembles popcorn in appearance and texture when popped. Kids are sure to appreciate these tasty cookies, especially after they enjoy watching the miniature grains popping in the pan.

Rice pudding has long been a favorite dessert, a comforting reminder of childhood. Creamy Arborio Rice Pudding (page 108) is the ultimate creamy pudding. Its consistency comes from a special short-grain Italian rice used for making risotto, a rice dish with the unique characteristic of creaminess. Do not use converted rice. The grains stay firm and won't cook down to the desired creamy consistency.

My true appreciation for rice was born during the years I lived in Asia. It was there I encountered glutinous sweet rice. In Japan, my son Todd and I pounded sweet rice, or mochi gome, into sticky, glutinous New Year's rice cakes. In Hong Kong, we ate it molded into an opulent rice pudding studded with candied fruits displayed like crown jewels. But my favorite way is from Thailand. Thai Coconut Rice Pudding with Mangoes and Macadamias (page 107) is the most delicious rice pudding you may ever taste. Admittedly rich, it is a wonderful way to splurge and create a dramatic ending for a special Southeast Asian meal.

Desserts are one way to work nutritious grains and vegetables into the diet. Wheat germ, whole-wheat flour and carrots boost the nutritional value of recipes such as Five-Spice Carrot Cake (page 106). If you must cut back on the amount of sugar and saturated fats in your diet, then leave off the icing and lightly sprinkle with powdered sugar. The moist, richly-flavored cake is so good, it can stand on its own.

HARLEQUIN SHORTBREAD

For a special gift, alternate vanilla and chocolate shortbread wedges in a gold tin lined with lavender tissue and paper lace. Before packing the shortbread, sift cocoa over the chocolate wedges and powdered sugar over the vanilla wedges. Gluten-free rice flour gives shortbread a melt-in-your-mouth texture. Purchase rice flour in health food stores, but do not use sweet rice flour from Asian markets in this recipe.

1 cup top-quality unsalted butter, room temperature (no substitute)
2/3 cup powdered sugar
1 teaspoon pure vanilla extract
1/4 teaspoon salt
1-1/2 cups soft-wheat, flour
1/2 cup rice flour
1 tablespoon unsweetened cocoa powder

Preheat oven to 275°F (135°C). In a medium-size bowl, cream butter and sugar with a wooden spoon. Blend in vanilla and salt. Add wheat flour and rice flour; stir until blended. Gather up dough; divide in half. To 1 half, gently knead in the cocoa. Pat each piece of dough, separately, into a 9-inch round, nonstick cake pan. Smooth the tops. Score each pan of dough neatly into 8 wedges. Lightly prick the tops. Bake 45 minutes or until crisp and dry. Do not allow shortbread to darken. Remove from oven; cut following scored lines. Cool completely. Carefully remove wedges from pans and alternate flavors on serving plates. Makes 16 wedges.

GINGERBREAD PUDDING

American colonists created a soft, cakelike gingerbread sweetened with molasses. This delicious version is like cake, yet has the moistness of pudding. It is made with whole-wheat pastry flour and rye flour, which are mainly used in breads. I like to drizzle tangy lemon sauce over each serving, then top with a spoonful of softly whipped cream.

1/2 cup whole-wheat pastry flour or whole-wheat flour
1/2 cup rye flour
1/2 teaspoon baking soda
1/2 teaspoon ground ginger
1/4 teaspoon each ground cloves, cinnamon, mace
1/4 teaspoon salt
1/2 cup butter or margarine, room temperature, cut into pieces
1/2 cup packed light brown sugar
1 large egg
1/2 cup molasses
1/2 cup boiling water

Generously grease a 9-inch-square baking pan. Preheat oven to 350°F (175°C). In a large bowl, sift together flours, soda, spices and salt. Set aside. In the large bowl of an electric mixer, cream butter and brown sugar. Beat in egg and molasses. Slowly add dry ingredients and boiling water. Blend at low speed, just until dry ingredients disappear. Scrape down side of bowl with a spatula. Pour into prepared pan. Bake on middle rack 25 to 30 minutes. Cool 10 minutes before spooning into serving dishes. Makes 6 to 8 servings.

FIVE-SPICE CARROT CAKE

Nutty-tasting wheat germ and fragrant spices with a hint of Chinese five-spice powder lend character to this moist, dark cake.

1 cup cooked, pureed carrots (2 large carrots)
3/4 cup vegetable oil
2 large eggs
1 teaspoon pure vanilla extract
2 tablespoons golden raisins
1 cup sugar
1/2 cup each soft-wheat flour and whole-wheat flour
1/4 cup wheat germ, lightly toasted
1 teaspoon each ground cinnamon and nutmeg
1 teaspoon baking soda
1/2 teaspoon salt
1/8 teaspoon five-spice powder or ground allspice
1-1/2 cup broken walnut halves

Orange Frosting:
3 tablespoons unsalted butter or margarine
1 (3-oz.) package cream cheese, room temperature
3 cups powdered sugar
1 tablespoon orange liqueur or orange juice
1 teaspoon grated orange peel

Preheat oven to 350°F (175°C). Butter and flour a deep, round 9-inch baking pan. In a large bowl, combine carrot puree, oil, eggs, vanilla and raisins. Into a medium-size bowl, sift remaining ingredients, except walnuts. Stir dry ingredients into carrot mixture just until blended. Pour into prepared pan. Bake 30 minutes or until the cake tests done. Cool 10 minutes; turn onto a serving plate. Frost cake; press walnuts evenly over the top and side. Makes 8 to 10 servings.

Orange Frosting
In a medium-size bowl, cream butter and cream cheese. Beat in remaining ingredients until smooth. Makes about 3 cups frosting.

Thai Coconut Rice Pudding with Mangoes & Macadamias

Sweet glutinous rice is commonly cooked in coconut milk throughout Southeast Asia. This sweet version is a favorite in Thailand, as well as with anyone outside of Thailand who tastes it. The addition of almond extract and macadamias is not traditional, but delicious, nonetheless. For convenience, use top-quality canned coconut milk from Thailand.

1 recipe Sweet Glutinous Rice (page 13)
1-1/2 cups unsweetened coconut milk, plus more if desired
1/3 to 1/2 cup sugar
1/4 teaspoon salt
1/4 teaspoon almond extract
Fresh sliced mangoes or other sliced fresh fruits
About 1/3 cup coarsely chopped macadamia nuts
Fresh tropical flowers

Rinse and soak rice as directed. Do not add water to the rice for steaming; instead pour in 3/4 cup coconut milk. Steam as directed. When rice is tender, stir in sugar, salt and almond extract. Pack rice into a small, oiled round bowl. Line a medium, flat bamboo basket with ti leaves or banana leaves. Unmold rice on basket. Arrange sliced mangoes around the base of the rice. Decorate top of rice with macadamia nuts. Decorate tray with fresh flowers. Spoon 1 or 2 tablespoons coconut milk over each portion of rice. Makes 6 servings.

CREAMY ARBORIO RICE PUDDING

Italian arborio rice makes the ultimate creamy rice pudding. Long, gentle cooking breaks down the starch in this short-grain rice, causing it to coagulate and become creamy. Keep the flavors simple, the finest vanilla you can buy and a hint of fresh lemon. If you like, add a dash of ground cinnamon or nutmeg and chopped toasted almonds or pistachios to the top.

1/2 cup Arborio rice or other short- or medium-grain rice
5 cups milk
1/2 cup sugar
3/4 teaspoon salt
Grated peel of 1 small lemon
2 tablespoons raisins
1 cup whipping cream, whipped
1 teaspoon pure vanilla extract

In the top pan of a double boiler, combine rice, milk, sugar and salt. Place over a double boiler bottom filled with gently simmering water. Cook pudding 1 hour, stirring after 30 minutes. Add the lemon peel and raisins. Cook 1 more hour, stirring several times. Pudding will begin to thicken after 1-1/2 hours. Replenish water in double boiler, as necessary. The pudding consistency will be soft, but will thicken upon cooling. Chill slightly; fold in whipped cream and vanilla. Spoon into serving dishes; refrigerate overnight. Makes 4 to 6 servings.

CHERRY-ALMOND GRANOLA COOKIES

*Nuts, dried fruit, chocolate and spice made these large, chewy cookies a big hit with
a TV crew I worked with on a holiday segment featuring gift-giving ideas from the kitchen.
Decorated with a lacy design of melted white chocolate, the cookies were irresistible!
Treat your friends to a basketful this year!*

2 cups all-purpose flour
1-1/2 teaspoons baking powder
1 teaspoon baking soda
1/2 teaspoon salt
1 teaspoon ground cinnamon
1/4 teaspoon each ground allspice, nutmeg and ginger
1/2 cup butter or margarine
1 cup packed light brown sugar
2 large eggs, room temperature
1-1/2 teaspoon vanilla extract
1 tablespoon almond liqueur, coffee liqueur, rum or milk
1-1/2 cups Cherry-Almond Granola (page 96)
3 ounces semisweet chocolate, coarsely chopped

Preheat oven to 300°F (150°C). Into a medium-size bowl, sift flour, baking powder, soda, salt and spices; set aside. Cream butter and sugar; beat in eggs. Stir in vanilla, liqueur, granola, chocolate and flour mixture. Place large spoonfuls of dough 2 inches apart on greased baking sheets. Bake 10 to 12 minutes, until golden-brown and puffy. Cool 3 minutes; remove from baking sheets. When completely cool, store in an airtight container. Makes about 18 cookies.

Rose Geranium Pound Cake

"Wait not till tomorrow; Gather the roses of life today," wrote Pierre de Ronsard. What could be more pleasurable than a slice of rose-scented pound cake, a pot of steaming-hot herb tea and the company of a good friend? The aroma and flavor of a single bite will remind you of simpler times and romantic, old fashioned rose gardens of days gone by.

1 cup soft-wheat flour
1/4 teaspoon baking soda
1/4 teaspoon baking powder
1/4 teaspoon salt
1/2 cup almond paste, crumbled
1/2 cup unsalted butter, room temperature
1 cup sugar
3 large eggs, room temperature
1/2 cup sour cream
3 or 4 small rose geranium leaves, minced (if available)

Preheat oven to 325°F (165°C). Grease and flour a 2-quart decorative baking pan with a tube. In a small bowl, sift flour, soda, baking powder and salt; set aside. In a medium-size bowl, cream almond paste with butter until smooth. Gradually beat in sugar. Add eggs, one at a time, beating well after each addition. Beat 2 minutes more, until batter is thick and creamy. Add half the sour cream and half the flour mixture. Beat on medium-low speed, until flour is incorporated. Add remaining sour cream and flour mixture. Beat just until flour disappears and batter is blended. Stir in rose geranium leaves, by hand. Spoon batter into prepared pan. Bake 30 minutes; reduce heat to 300°F (150°C). Bake 20 minutes or until a wooden pick inserted in center comes out clean. Cool 15 minutes; remove from pan while warm. Makes 1 cake.

Aztec Cookies with Amaranth

These crunchy little cookies will melt in your mouth. They are similar to nut-filled Mexican wedding cakes, except they are made with delicate popped amaranth, the "mystical grain of the Aztecs." Aztec women baked amaranth into cakes shaped like birds, snakes and animals.

3 tablespoons Popped Amaranth (page 23)
1 cup butter, room temperature
1/2 cup powdered sugar, plus more for dusting
1/2 teaspoon pure vanilla extract
1 teaspoon pure almond extract
2 cups all-purpose flour
1/2 teaspoon baking soda
1/8 teaspoon salt

Preheat oven to 350°F (175°C). Prepare Popped Amaranth. In a medium-size bowl, cream butter and sugar with a wooden spoon. Stir in vanilla and almond extract. In a medium-size bowl, sift flour, soda and salt. Stir amaranth and flour mixture into the butter mixture until a dough is formed. Shape into balls, using 1 tablespoon dough per cookie. Place cookies on a baking sheet. Bake 10 to 12 minutes or until lightly browned on the bottom. Sift powdered sugar over warm cookies. Makes about 28 cookies.

Variation
For a crunchy coating, roll unbaked dough balls in 2-1/2 tablespoons Popped Amaranth and omit dusting cookies with powdered sugar.

Glossary of Ingredients

Wheat

Wheat Berries: Husked, whole wheat kernels are surrounded by a layer of bran. They must be soaked and cooked in liquid to become digestible. Cooked wheat berries and sprouted wheat berries add texture and flavor to breads. Wheat berries are highly nutritious; they are rich in protein, carbohydrates, B vitamins and amino acids. One cup of cooked wheat berries has about 110 calories.

Cracked Wheat: Uncooked wheat berries are cracked into fine, medium or coarse grinds. Cracked wheat must be boiled in liquid for a lengthy period before using; presoaking speeds the process. Coarse grinds are good for pilaf, salad, soup and cereal.

Bulgur Wheat: For centuries, Middle Eastern women boiled wheat berries, dried them in the hot sun on flat baskets, then stone ground the parched wheat into coarse, medium or fine bulgur. The coarse grind is good for pilaf; medium grind for salads. Add finely ground bulgur to breads or make porridge with it. Bulgur has a nutty, delicious flavor. Unlike its cousin, cracked wheat, bulgur cooks quickly and can be soaked, simmered briefly or steamed. It is rich in protein with generous amounts of calcium, iron, thiamine, riboflavin and niacin.

Couscous: Couscous is not a type of grain, but is made from the endosperm of refined durum wheat or semolina. Although served like a grain, it cooks more quickly and is lighter than any grain. Couscous is the national dish of the Maghreb, the North African countries of Algeria, Tunisia and Morocco, but associations are found in Brazil, France and Italy. Couscous is traditionally cooked in steam over broth or a savory stew, not immersed in liquid.

Wheat Bran: Bran is the outer cover of the wheat kernel. It is composed of the six protective layers of the wheat berry. It contains indigestible cellulose and is an excellent source of fiber in the diet. Besides fiber, bran adds flavor and nutrients to breads and other dishes.

Wheat Germ: Wheat germ is the embryo of the wheat kernel. Nutritionally, the best part, it is an excellent source of B vitamins. The germ contains oils, which makes it susceptible to rancidity. Refrigerate after opening. Wheat germ adds a nutty flavor to foods such as meat loaf, breads, cakes and pastries.

Wheat Flakes: Can be used in baking.

Rice

Rice is a grass. When the husk is removed, you have brown rice. White rice is produced when the brown rice is polished to remove the bran and germ. Rice is classified as long-grain, medium-grain and short-grain. Long-grain rice and medium-grain rice are generally interchangeable in recipes. Do not substitute them for stickier short-grain rice. Rice expands at least twice in size when cooked.

Long-Grain Rice: Indica rice cooks into separate, dry grains. Most rice grown in the Southern United States is long-grain. It cooks up fluffy because it contains amylose, a protein starch which causes cooked rice to harden in the refrigerator. This process is called retrogradation, in which the cells collapse, squeezing out moisture. The effects are negated when the rice is heated. Rice is enriched with thiamine, niacin and iron and sometimes calcium, riboflavin and vitamin D. White rice is also higher in thiamine and iron than brown rice.

Medium-Grain Rice: Most Japanese- and Korean-Americans prefer cooking with medium-grain Japonica rice, which has short, moist grains and a more pronounced taste. This rice grows in the temperate climates found in California, Spain and Italy. It contains the protein amylopectin, a waxy substance which causes cohesion. Medium-grain rice cooks in the same time as long grain, but requires less liquid. Purchase California medium-grain rice in Asian markets under the names Nishiki, Kiku, Tsuru Mai, New Rose, Miyako Calrose and Hinode® Calrose. Valencia is a Spanish medium-grain rice available at Hispanic markets.

Short-Grain Rice: Short-grain Japonica rice has a high level of amylopectin, making it very cohesive. California growers ship most of the grain to Puerto Rico or sell it to American cereal manufacturers. Large amounts go to Puerto Rican and Cuban communities in New York and Miami. There is less demand for short-grain rice in the United States because of the great success of medium-grain rice. Short-grain is the table rice of choice in Japan. One California short-grain is Silver Pearl™. Thai and Japanese black rice are also available in some Asian markets. Italian arborio is used for risotto.

Sweet Glutinous Rice: This Japonica rice has the highest level of amylopectin, causing the cooked grains to lose their shape. The grains will not harden upon standing. It is eaten in China, Japan, Thailand, Laos and Cambodia. Glutinous rice contains no gluten. Although sweet rice grown in

California is not coated with starch, it still needs rinsing. It is used to make rice cakes, dumplings, savory stuffings, soups and sweet rice wine.

Converted Rice: Converted or "parboiled" white rice retains some of its nutrients through a steam pressure process before milling. However, the grains take longer to cook than regular long-grain and harden upon standing. This process has long been used in India to keep rice from falling apart during cooking.

Instant Rice: Rice which is partially cooked then dehydrated. The appearance and texture of the cooked rice grains are altered. This rice contains the fewest nutrients of all the rice forms.

Specialty Rices

Arborio: Northern Italy produces arborio short-grain rice, which is one of several strains used exclusively to make the classic dish risotto. When cooked, arborio absorbs liquid slowly while its starches form the creamy, binding sauce that distinguishes the dish. Arborio rice has the ability to hold its shape during the cooking process, even though it is short-grain and very starchy. Look for arborio "superfino," which indicates that the grains are large. Cooking experts have tested California long- and medium-grain rice for risotto and reported favorable results.

Basmati: The "queen of fragrance," this aromatic long-grain rice grows best in the Himalayan foothills due to unique climatic and geographic factors. It is the favored rice of India and Pakistan. The special scent is released from the rice's endosperm when it is cooked. Its flavor is unmatched by any other rice. Basmati is aged and dried for a long period to remove moisture and enhance the fragrance. It doubles in length when cooked, yet stays about the same in thickness. It is essential to rinse and soak basmati before cooking. When shopping for rice in Indian markets look for dehradoon, Punjab basmati, or the more assertive basmati from Pakistan.

Jasmine: Long-grain jasmine rice from Thailand is an only slightly cohesive rice. It has an exquisite faint floral bouquet. Jasmine is my favorite rice for Asian recipes calling for long-grain rice. It is especially good for fried rice. Purchase jasmine from Asian markets in bags marked "from Thailand." Jasmati™ Rice, a jasmine-type rice is grown in Texas, has a sweet, enticing aroma and subtle flavor. This soft-textured rice is excellent for Oriental dishes and desserts.

Texmati® Rice: Also called American basmati. This Texas rice, a hybrid of Indian basmati and long-grain American rice, has an appetizing popcorn aroma and a subtle nutty taste. Texmati combines some of the flavor of basmati with the cooking characteristics of American rice. It is not necessary to rinse or soak this rice before cooking. It cooks in about fifteen minutes. When cooked, Texmati elongates 50%; the grains stay separate and fluffy.

Brown Rices

Brown Rice: Brown rice consists of the whole rice kernel with only the outer husk removed. The unpolished grain retains the bran layer which gives this rice its characteristic chewy texture. Nutty-tasting brown rice take about 45 minutes to become tender. Decrease the cooking time by soaking the rice several hours. Brown rice is slightly more nutritious than enriched white rice and adds valuable fiber to the diet. It is available in long-, medium- or short-grains. Cooked long-grain brown rice dries out and becomes hard rather quickly. Short-grain brown rice stays moist longer after cooking.

Texmati Lite Bran® Rice: This brown rice is lightly milled to leave a thin portion of the nutritious bran layer on the grain. Lite Bran retains 90% of the nutritional value of Texmati brown rice and 50% of the bran content. Best of all, it cooks in half the time of regular brown rice, about 25 minutes.

Konriko® Wild Pecan® Rice: This rice is the result of cross-breeding a strain from French Indochina and an American high-yield, long-grain seed. The rice has a subtle pecanlike flavor and nutty aroma. About 90% of the bran is left on the grain yet the rice cooks in only 25 minutes. It is more delicate than regular brown rice.

Wehani®: Aromatic rust-colored rice developed by the California Lundberg brothers who pioneered the cultivation of organic rice. Some say the taste is reminiscent of roasted chestnuts.

Riz Cous: Created by the Lundberg Brothers, Riz Cous consists of broken particles of California brown rice which resemble couscous before and after cooking. It is a delicious and useful substitute for couscous.

Wild Rice: The wild seed of an aquatic grass native to the Native Americans. Eaten like grain, wild rice is not a true cereal grain. A staple food of the Indians, earthy-flavored wild rice has character and body. Minnesota law decrees that wild rice be harvested with traditional harvesting sticks. The rice is fermented up to two weeks to develop the flavor and facilitate hulling. Wild rice cooks in 45 to 60 minutes, and splits properly when fully cooked. Wild rice can be cooked with other grains, and is especially good with game birds and poultry.

Other Grains

Amaranth: Ancient amaranth was the prized crop of the Aztecs. It grows and thrives in adverse conditions. The tiny seeds resemble poppy seeds; up to 500 may appear on one seed head. Amaranth is rich in iron and high in calcium. Amaranth presents the cook with a glutinous challenge; the seeds cook into a porridgelike mixture. Mix cooked amaranth into soups, cookies, breads and casserole dishes. Leftover chilled amaranth can be sautéed in butter like polenta.

Barley: Barley, used as Sumerian money 4,000 years ago, enriches the soups and dark breads of Europe today. It is malted for brewing beer and for malted milkshakes. Whole, hulled barley must be soaked several hours before cooking. It has so much tough hull and bran, the milling process leaves only a small "pearl," or endosperm, of polished barley behind. Lightly pearled, semi-hulled barley is more flavorful and nutritious, but not always available. Hato mugi, or pressed barley, is used in Japanese and macrobiotic cuisine. Barley is a chewy and satisfying grain which can be combined with other grains or legumes.

Buckwheat: Buckwheat is classified as a fruit, not a cereal grain. It contains high amounts of all eight essential amino acids, including lysine the building blocks of protein. It is high in potassium and phosphorus and contains 50% more vitamin B than wheat. Buckwheat is a food of the people. Buckwheat pancakes have long been an American favorite. In Russia, roasted groats are called kasha. Eastern and Western Europe consider buckwheat a food staple. In Japan, soba, or buckwheat, is a vital food source used to make noodles and dumplings. Prepare the groats as a side dish or add to soups, dumplings and meat stuffings. White untoasted groats have a milder flavor than kasha. Purchase the groats and flour in health food stores. One cup cooked plain kasha contains slightly less than 200 calories.

Corn: "Maize" is indigenous to North America and has multiple food uses. Sweet table corn is eaten as a vegetable. Field corn is made into corn oil, corn syrup, popcorn, cornmeal, hominy and cornstarch. Blue Indian corn is ground into meal.

Grits: Coarsely ground, hulled kernels of mature dried white or yellow corn. Most supermarket grits cook up into a smooth, white cereal in eight to ten minutes, although directions often recommend longer cooking. Stone-ground grits have a coarse texture which can vary from mill to mill. They have a superior corn taste, contain no preservatives, and are often speckled with the nutritious germ of the corn. Stone-ground grits take about 25 minutes to cook. Taste several kinds of grits to determine which you like best All grits are enriched with vitamins and minerals.

Hominy: Polished white or yellow corn soaked in a 2% lye solution or slaked (hydrated) lime to soften the hull and swell the grains. Hominy is popular in the South; in Mexican cuisine it is known as posole. Posole also refers to a dish of hominy and pork. Hominy is a fairly rich source of minerals. It is available canned, dried or frozen. Dried hominy must be soaked overnight and simmered at least two hours. Dried hominy is ground to make grits.

Kamut: This ricelike ancient grain was a favorite of the pharaohs. "Kamut" is the Egyptian name for wheat. The grain evolved in the fertile crescent area around 4000 B.C., and is still grown in the Northern Mediterranean region. Its nutritional value is higher than that of hybridized wheat. Kamut is high in protein, potassium, zinc and magnesium. Kamut flour, cereals, pasta and baked goods made from kamut are available at health food stores. Kamut triples in volume when cooked. Because it is ricelike in appearance, I like to mix cooked kamut into rice dishes.

Millet: In China, millet was the staple before rice became predominant. It is a major food crop in Africa and India. Sometimes referred to as the poor man's rice, millet is high in protein, and has generous amounts of iron, vitamins and minerals. The grain can be cooked and eaten like rice. It makes a good side dish for spicy meats and sauces. A small amount of toasted, soaked millet adds texture and flavor to breads. Ground millet can be added to breads like cornmeal. One cup cooked millet has 90 calories. Purchase hulled millet at health food stores.

Oats: Oats are rich in protein and minerals. Oat groats are the hulled, whole grain. The groats are steamed and flattened for making the familiar rolled oats we eat in our breakfast porridge. Steel-cut oats are more coarse and labeled "Irish oatmeal." Quick-cooking oats are cut into smaller pieces. Soak oats before using in bread doughs. Make an interesting oat flour for breads by grinding the oats in the food processor.

Polenta: In Northern Italy, coarsely ground yellow or white cornmeal is made into polenta, a savory cornmeal pudding eaten instead of pasta. It can be served hot with butter or poured into a dish, cooled, sliced and sautéed in butter or oil. Polenta slices can be layered with meat sauce, then baked. Similar cornmeal mush puddings are eaten around the world.

Quinoa: (Keen-wa) Botanically, quinoa is not a true grain, although it is used as one. It is of the Chenopodium, or goose foot, family which includes spinach and beets. A staple of the ancient Incas, it is one of the most superior sources of protein in the vegetable world. The tiny seeds contain levels of all the essential amino acids, the building blocks of proteins, including lysine, which is scarce in most plant proteins. Quinoa is high in calcium, iron, vitamins B, E and potassium. Quinoa seeds are coated with a bitter-tasting substance called saponin which acts as a natural pesticide. Although processed quinoa is well-rinsed, it is a good idea to rinse it again in your own kitchen. Saponin creates a soap-like foam in water. Pale-colored, sweet-tasting altiplano quinoa is the best strain available as well as the most expensive.

Rye: Popular in Eastern Europe, rye resembles wheat in appearance but has a heartier flavor. It is used in breads and in whiskey distillation. As a side dish, it is best mixed with another grain such as rice. Flaked rye is good in granola, and can be eaten as cereal like rolled oats. Prepare rye berries like wheat berries; soak overnight, then simmer until tender. Rye sprouts add chewiness and flavor to breads. Try cracked rye in split-pea soup.

Sorghum: Similar to millet, ancient sorghum is a staple grain in Africa. It is used in Eastern Europe to make black breads. Cook sorghum as a breakfast cereal or add to rice. Cook one cup sorghum and a pinch of salt in four cups water for one hour. Sorghum came to America from Africa. The grain is fed to cattle and the stalks are used to make sorghum molasses.

Spelt: Spelt is an ancient relative of wheat. Mentioned several times in the Bible, it was grown in Mesopotamia more than 9,000 years ago. In Ezekiel 4:9, the prophet Ezekiel was instructed to make a bread that included spelt. A longtime favorite in Europe, it is now appearing in American kitchens. Spelt contains more protein than wheat. It can be dressed with a salad dressing, tossed into soups, chili or stews. Soak spelt grains overnight before cooking.

Teff: Teff is an important cereal grain staple in Ethiopia. Ancient teff seeds have been found in the Egyptian pyramids dating back to over 3000 B.C. Teff is a powerhouse of nutrition; especially high in iron and calcium. Teff is highly digestible. Red and brown teff have a rich nutty flavor and make an excellent hot breakfast cereal.

Flour
Wheat Flours

Whole-Wheat Flour: Milled from the wheat berry of hard winter wheat. The bran, germ and nutrients are intact. Bread made from 100% whole-wheat flour has a dense texture and a limited rise. The sticky dough will need additional kneading. Whole-wheat flour mixed with 50% white flour makes a dough which is easier to handle; the bread will be lighter with a good texture. Oils in the germ oxidize, causing the flour to become rancid; keep refrigerated. Graham flour is a type of coarse whole-wheat flour.

Whole-Wheat Pastry Flour: This whole-wheat flour is milled to a fine texture. Low in gluten, it is excellent for cakes, quick breads and pastries. A small portion of whole-wheat pastry flour adds tenderness to breads.

All-Purpose Flour: To make all-purpose flour, wheat berries are milled to separate the endosperm from bran and germ. The endosperm is ground into white flour. Bleaching agents chemically whiten most flour, speeding up the maturation process necessary for a flour with good baking qualities. Unbleached flour, good for yeast bread, is aged naturally and has a creamy hue. The two are interchangeable. All-purpose flour is a medium-strength blend of soft and hard wheat flours which can be used in yeast bread, cake or pastry. Higher-protein flour is best for yeast bread; read the bag labels and buy all-purpose flour with eleven grams of protein per cup (4 oz.), or more. Select a lower-protein flour with ten grams per cup or less, for cakes and quick breads. Make a substitute, low-protein cake flour by combining three parts sifted all-purpose flour to one part cornstarch.

Bread Flour: Made from hard wheat, bread flour is similar to all-purpose flour, but has a higher gluten or protein content (14 grams per cup), and is excellent for yeast breads. It is especially good for blending with low-protein flours. You may need less of this flour in your bread recipes because it requires a bit more liquid. Be sure and knead bread flour doughs well.

Soft-Wheat Flour: This low-protein flour contains nine grams of protein per cup. Made from 100% soft winter wheat, it is excellent for cakes, biscuits, pastries and quick breads. Soft-wheat flour is readily available in Southern grocery stores and through mail order.

Cake Flour: This high-starch, low-protein flour contains six to eight grams of protein per cup. It gives cakes a fine grain and texture. Sift before using; fine cake flour lumps easily. Pastry flour contains eight to nine grams of protein per cup and is excellent for pastries.

Self-Rising Flour: One cup of this commercial blend is mixed with one and one-half teaspoons baking powder and one-half teaspoon salt. It is especially popular in the South for making biscuits.

Semolina Flour: Granular, high-protein semolina is made from cold-weather, hard durum wheat. Its primary use is for commercially dried pasta and couscous. The high gluten content enables the pasta to hold together while boiling. Granular, enriched semolina (sometimes labeled pasta flour) is available in supermarkets. Semolina can also be found in Italian, Indian and Middle Eastern markets. Use for pasta, puddings, dumplings, as a coating for fried foods and to thicken sauces or soups. Substitute at least half regular flour for semolina in baking. Semolina is delicious cooked like polenta and flavored with butter and cheese.

Panocha: A flour ground from sprouted wheat. Popular in Mexican holiday baked goods, it is available in Southwestern and Latin markets.

Other Flours & Meals

Amaranth Flour: Many commercial foods such as cookies, cereals and graham crackers contain small amounts of high-protein amaranth flour. The flour contains no gluten and has a pleasant taste. It is excellent for people with grain sensitivities.

Barley Flour: Low-gluten barley flour is a soft starch, excellent for baking. The whitish flour gives baked goods a grayish color. Use about 20% barley flour mixed with wheat flour for baked goods with a soft dense texture. Toast the flour before using to enhance the flavor.

Buckwheat Flour: Buckwheat flour has a more distinctive flavor than wheat flour. It is commonly used for making Japanese soba noodles, Russian blinis, Breton crêpes and American pancakes. Substitute three to four tablespoons buckwheat flour per cup of wheat flour.

Cornmeal: Dried from ground corn, cornmeal or "Indian meal" was first used by the Native Americans for making breads. Cajuns fry cornmeal mush in bacon fat to make a thick, crusty breakfast porridge. White cornmeal is favored in the South; yellow cornmeal in the North. Blue and red cornmeal, made from Indian corn, are popular in the Southwest. Slightly grainier than white or yellow meal, they are made into tortillas, breads and corn chips. Blue cornmeal is readily available in gourmet markets and health food stores. Stone-ground meals are made from the whole grain and are more nutritious.

Corn Flour: Dried corn is ground into a fine meal, almost like flour. It is used in the South as a coating for fried fish.

Cornstarch: Ground from the heart of the corn kernel, cornstarch is a pure starch. It is used as a thickener for sauces or soups and can be added to flour in baking.

Masa Harina de Maiz: A special dried, treated meal made from slaked corn or posole (hominy). The corn is treated with a lime-water solution, ground and dried. It is used for making tortillas, tamales and even breads. Regular cornmeal is not a substitute.

Quinoa Flour: The seeds are ground into gluten-free flour, which is used to enrich baked goods, cooked into a porridge or used as a thickener.

Rice Flour: Made from finely ground, cooked white or brown rice. Gluten free, it is excellent for making shortbread, sauces and for coating foods. Sweet glutinous rice flour is also gluten free, and made from sweet glutinous rice. It is used for making Asian dumplings and pastries and a quick version of the Japanese pounded rice snack, mochi. The two flours are not interchangeable.

Rye Flour: Dark rye flour and medium rye flour are excellent for breadmaking. Medium rye is a mixture of light and dark flour, most often found in supermarkets. Blend rye flour with wheat flour to make a better loaf. Try this formula: replace one-fourth cup of each measured cup of wheat flour with one-fourth cup rye flour. Do not use more than 50% rye flour. The more rye flour, the lower the volume of the bread. Certain pumpernickel breads are made from 100% rye flour. Commercial dark rye bread gets its color from caramel or burnt sugar.

Teff Flour: Used to make the crepelike Ethiopian bread, *injera*, made from a fermented batter with a spongelike consistency. It is excellent for making quick breads, pancakes and for thickening soups. White teff is good for making delicate cakes and pastries. In baking, add 20% teff to wheat flour.

Triticale Flour: Triticale is milled from a man-made grain developed in Sweden in the late 1950s. A hybrid of wheat and rye, it is slightly higher in protein than wheat, and contains a generous amount of the essential acid, lysine. Triticale is low in gluten. Use nutty-tasting triticale flour like wheat or rye flour. Allow the breads one rising. Breads may need a longer cooking period. Replace one-third cup of each measured cup of wheat flour with one-third cup triticale flour.

Other Ingredients

Barley Malt Syrup: Rich, dark, sticky grain syrup with a strong taste like molasses but not as strong as blackstrap molasses. It is extracted from sprouted, roasted whole barley. This complex sugar is slowly converted by the body into energy. Beer results when you mix the syrup with hops, then ferment the mixture with yeasts. Store syrup in a cool place; if fermentation occurs, refrigerate or discard if the odor becomes too strong. Purchase in health food stores. Use in baking, toppings or as a glaze.

Butter: High-quality unsalted butter is indispensable for fine baking and cooking. The top grades contain less water than salted butter. Valued for its delicate flavor, refrigerate unsalted butter in a covered container away from strong odors. Freeze for long storage. Although the flavor will not be the same, top-quality margarine can be substituted for butter in many of the recipes. For some recipes, such as shortbread, there is no flavor substitute for butter. If margarine is used, shortbread tends to spread too much.

Cassia Bark: A pungent, flavorful Asian cinnamon with a thick bark.

Garlic: Select plump, firm, large heads of garlic, preferably from ethnic markets or farmer's markets. Smash the cloves with the flat side of a large knife blade to easily remove the peels. The flavor of garlic changes depending upon its use. Crushed garlic has a more intense flavor than the sliced or whole cloves. When added at the beginning of the dish, garlic has a milder flavor which blends well with the other ingredients. When quickly sautéed, garlic has a more distinctive flavor and aroma. Never allow garlic to turn dark brown or burn; the flavor and possibly the dish will be ruined.

Golden Syrup: This rich golden syrup is a by-product of sugar refining. It has been boiled until no more sugar crystals appear. The British brand, Lyle's Golden Syrup, can be found in the gourmet sections of grocery stores and specialty markets. It is interchangeable with light-colored corn syrup.

Green Onions: Also called scallions. Look for small, tender green onions as opposed to large green onions, which may have tougher fibers and a stronger flavor. Trim off the root end, then smash the onion flat with the broad side of a large knife or cleaver for easy mincing. Store in an airtight plastic bag in the refrigerator several days.

Herbs: Fresh herbs add intense flavor and color to foods. All herbs are best used fresh, especially basil, cilantro, mint and parsley. Italian flat-leaf parsley is particularly flavorful. The dried form of these herbs is not an acceptable substitute for fresh herbs. Some herbs such as bay leaves, dry well and are suitable for cooking. Dried rosemary and oregano have an intense flavor; add in smaller amounts than fresh herbs. If substituting dried herbs for fresh, use one-third the amount of dried herbs. Never use old, musty dried herbs. Store dried herbs in a cool, dry place.

Ground Pepper: Ground black pepper comes from dried black peppercorns of the tropical *Piper nigrum* vine. For the best flavor, grind your own black peppercorns in a pepper mill. Finely ground and coarsely ground black peppers are available in the spice sections of supermarkets.

Rice Syrup: This mild, sweet, healthful syrup, made from white or brown rice, is an excellent substitute for corn syrup. Brown rice syrup contains more B vitamins and minerals. Organic brown rice syrup has a rich flavor, reminiscent of butterscotch. Purchase in natural health food stores. Store on a cool shelf; heat the jar in warm water if crystallization occurs. Use in baking, toppings or as a glaze.

Salt: Salt helps blend the individual flavors in a dish. Table salt is combined with sodium carbonate for easy flowing. It is a fine-grained salt with a salty, intense flavor. Sea salt has larger crystals and is less salty tasting. Kosher salt has a coarse texture and a milder flavor than sea salt or table salt. Sea salt and kosher salts are manufactured without additives. They can be used to season dishes in place of table salt; add to taste.

Soy Sauce: Soy sauce is a dark seasoning liquid made from a fermented soybean and wheat mash. Amino acids formed from soybean protein are natural components which heighten the taste sensations and enhance the flavor of foods. For Chinese dishes, use Pearl River Bridge, "Superior" soy sauce found in most Asian markets. Chinese soy sauce isn't compatible with the delicate flavors of Japanese cooking. Use top-quality Japanese soy sauce such as Kikkoman, which can also be used in preparing dishes from other Asian cultures. Refrigerate low-sodium soy sauce after opening. Do not substitute chemically fermented domestic soy sauces for naturally brewed soy sauce. Light or thin soy sauce is saltier than medium soy; good for preserving the light colors of foods.

Sun-dried Tomato Paste: A rich-tasting concentrate made from sun-dried tomatoes. It is available in tubes from fine food stores; use what you need and keep the rest refrigerated. Make your own paste by simmering packaged, dried tomato halves in a little water until soft. Puree in the food processor with some of the cooking liquid to facilitate blending.

Tofu: A white custardlike food made from coagulated soy milk. Tofu is an important protein source in Asia. It is rich in vitamins, minerals and important amino acids. Firm Chinese-style tofu is excellent for frying. Regular Japanese-style tofu should be firmed up before frying; wrap in paper towels and press to remove liquid. Purchase the freshest tofu from tubs of water in Asian markets. In supermarkets, look for chilled packages of tofu with clear packing water. Notice the pull-date for quality control; do not purchase out of date tofu. At home, rinse tofu by submerging it in cool water. Refrigerate up to seven days, changing the water daily. Blanch older tofu in boiling water; use in dishes which require cooking.

Vegetable Oils: Use light-bodied, extra-virgin olive oil for salads and fish dishes; heavier-bodied extra-virgin olive oil can be used for sautéeing, brushing over grilled foods or drizzling over cooked dishes. Use only the freshest olive oil; store in a cool place. Top-quality peanut oil, corn oil and canola oil are excellent for stir-frying and deep-frying. Safflower oil has the highest level of linoleic acid; a property which helps lower blood cholesterol levels. Sesame seed oil is used as a perfume; add in small amounts to flavor foods. Look for Japanese brands which are of higher quality. Purchase in small amounts; store in a cool place. Always use the freshest oils for cooking.

Mail Order Addresses

Organically raised grains, beans, seeds and nuts including amaranth and quinoa: Arrowhead Mills, P.O. Box 2059, Herford, TX 79045-2059, (806) 364-8522. Catalog available.

Quinoa, kamut organic pasta: Eden Foods, Inc., 701 Tecumseh Road, Clinton, MI 49236. Write for product information, recipes, organic standards and retail sources.

Texmati White Rice, Texmati Brown, Texmati Lite-Bran Rice, Royal Blend (white and brown blend) Gift Pak sampler $16.50. Send a check or credit card number. The pack provides a sample of all rice mentioned above: Farms of Texas, P.O. Box 1305, Alvin, TX 77512, (713) 331-8245.

Ellis Stansel's "popcorn" rice: Ellis Stansel, P.O. Box 206, Gueydan, LA 70542, (318) 536-6140.

Organically grown aromatic rice, Wehani rice, sushi rice, Riz Cous, brown rice blends, award-winning Black Japonica™ rice: Lundberg Family Farms, 5370 Church Street, Richvale, CA 95974, (916) 882-4551.

Valencia Rice: G.B. Ratto & Company, 821 Washington Street, Oakland, CA 94607, (800) 325-3483.

Stone-ground white grits, white and yellow corn meal, buckwheat flour, oat flour, rye meal, rice flour: Falls Mill and Country Store, Route 1, Box 44, Belvidere, TN 37306, (615) 469-7176.

Konriko® Wild Pecan® Rice: Conrad Rice Mill Inc., 307 Ann Street, P.O. Box 10640, New Iberia, LA 70562-0640, (318) 365-5806 or (800) 551-3245. Catalog available of specialty rice products, Cajun spices, rice cakes, bean soups.

Fresh stone-ground grits, cornmeal and corn flour: Hoppin' John's, 30 Pinckney Street, Charleston, SC 29401, (803) 577-6404.

White Lily Self-Rising Cornmeal Mix or Buttermilk Cornmeal Mix and Southern soft-wheat flours for biscuits, cakes and pastries. White Lily Unbleached, Bromated Bread Flour for yeast-raised baked goods: White Lily Foods Company, P.O. Box 871, Knoxville, TN 37901. Ask for a price list.

Sushi rice, large selection of flours, grains, cereals, including amaranth: Walnut Acres, Penns Creek, PA 17862, (717) 837-3874. Catalog available.

Blue cornmeal, blue corn tostaditas, chiles, posole: Los Chileros de Nuevo Mexico, P.O. Box 6215, Santa Fe, NM 87502, (505) 471-6967.

Triticale Flour, other flours and whole grains: Rosewood Market, 2803 Rosewood Drive, Columbia, SC 29205.

Metric Chart

Liquid Measure to Milliliters		
1/4 teaspoon	=	1.25 milliliters
1/2 teaspoon	=	2.5 milliliters
3/4 teaspoon	=	3.75 milliliters
1 teaspoon	=	5.0 milliliters
1-1/4 teaspoons	=	6.25 milliliters
1-1/2 teaspoons	=	7.5 milliliters
1-3/4 teaspoons	=	8.75 milliliters
2 teaspoons	=	10.0 milliliters
1 tablespoon	=	15.0 milliliters
2 tablespoons	=	30.0 milliliters

Fahrenheit to Celsius	
F	C
200—205	95
220—225	105
245—250	120
275	135
300—305	150
325—330	165
345—350	175
370—375	190
400—405	205
425—430	220
445—450	230
470—475	245
500	260

Liquid Measure to Liters		
1/4 cup	=	0.06 liters
1/2 cup	=	0.12 liters
3/4 cup	=	0.18 liters
1 cup	=	0.24 liters
1-1/4 cups	=	0.3 liters
1-1/2 cups	=	0.36 liters
2 cups	=	0.48 liters
2-1/2 cups	=	0.6 liters
3 cups	=	0.72 liters
3-1/2 cups	=	0.84 liters
4 cups	=	0.96 liters
4-1/2 cups	=	1.08 liters
5 cups	=	1.2 liters
5-1/2 cups	=	1.32 liters

Index